I0012326

Table of Contents

Chapter 1: Introduction to HTML 1

1.1 What is HTML?...1

    HTML Basics 1

    Structure of an HTML Document..1

    Semantic HTML 2

1.2 The History of HTML...2

    HTML in the Early Days 2

    The Browser Wars and HTML 3.2...2

    HTML 4.01 and XHTML 2

    The Arrival of HTML5..3

    Ongoing Evolution 3

1.3 HTML vs. XHTML 3

    HTML (Hypertext Markup Language) 3

    XHTML (Extensible Hypertext Markup Language) 3

    Key Differences 4

    Choosing Between HTML and XHTML..4

1.4 Anatomy of an HTML Document..4

    Document Type Declaration...5

    HTML Element..5

    Head Section 5

    Body Section 5

    Comments..6

1.5 Tools for HTML Development...6

    1. Text Editors..6

    2. Integrated Development Environments (IDEs) 7

    3. Browsers and Developer Tools 7

    4. Version Control Systems 7

    5. Package Managers...8

    6. Code Validators 8

    7. Code Editors for Collaboration 8

    8. Frameworks and Libraries 8

    9. Web Hosting and Deployment Services...8

Chapter 2: Setting Up Your HTML Environment...9

2.1 Choosing a Text Editor 9

Considerations for Choosing a Text Editor 9

Popular Text Editors for HTML Development...9

2.2 Installing a Web Browser 10

Default Web Browsers..10

Browser Testing...10

Mobile Browsers 11

Keeping Browsers Updated...11

2.3 Setting Up a Local Development Server..11

Why Use a Local Development Server?...11

Setting Up a Local Development Server..12

Using a Local Development Server 13

2.4 Creating Your First HTML Document..13

Step 1: Open a Text Editor...13

Step 2: Create the HTML Structure 14

Step 3: Add Content..14

Step 4: Save Your HTML File..14

Step 5: View Your Web Page 15

2.5 Validating Your HTML Code...15

Why HTML Validation Matters 15

How to Validate HTML Code..15

Interpreting Validation Results..16

Fixing Validation Issues..17

Chapter 3: Basic HTML Structure..18

3.1 HTML Document Structure...18

The Anatomy of an HTML Element...18

The Basic Structure of an HTML Document..18

3.2 HTML Elements and Tags...19

1. Headings (<h1> to <h6>)..19

2. Paragraphs (<p>)...20

3. Links (<a>) 20

4. Lists (<ul>, <ol>, and <li>)...20

5. Images (<img>) 20

6. Links to Local Resources (`<a>` with `href`)..20

7. Line Breaks (`<br>`) 20

8. Horizontal Lines (`<hr>`)...21

9. Comments (`<!-- -->`)...21

3.3 Headings and Paragraphs...21

Headings (`<h1>` to `<h6>`) 21

Paragraphs (`<p>`)...22

Combining Headings and Paragraphs 22

Styling Headings and Paragraphs with CSS..22

3.4 Lists and Links...23

Ordered Lists (`<ol>`) and List Items (`<li>`) 23

Unordered Lists (`<ul>`) and List Items (`<li>`) 24

Hyperlinks (`<a>`)..24

Linking to Local Resources..24

Linking to Email Addresses..24

Linking to Specific Sections of a Page 25

3.5 Comments in HTML 25

Syntax of HTML Comments..25

Using Comments for Documentation...25

Commenting Out Code..26

Conditional Comments..26

Best Practices for Using HTML Comments 26

Chapter 4: Text Formatting and Styling 28

4.1 Formatting Text with HTML 28

1. Bold Text (`<strong>`)..28

2. Italic Text (`<em>`) 28

3. Underlined Text (`<u>`)...28

4. Strikethrough Text (`<s>`) 28

5. Subscript and Superscript Text (`<sub>` and `<sup>`)..29

6. Marked Text (`<mark>`) 29

7. Abbreviations and Acronyms (`<abbr>`) 29

4.2 Working with Fonts and Colors 29

Setting Fonts with CSS..29

Setting Text Colors with CSS...30

Combining Font Styles and Colors 32

4.3 CSS for Styling HTML..32

Understanding CSS Syntax...32

CSS Selectors...33

Applying CSS Styles...33

Common CSS Properties..34

CSS Box Model...34

CSS Specificity 34

4.4 Text Alignment and Spacing...34

Text Alignment 34

Line Height 35

Letter Spacing 35

Word Spacing 35

Text Indentation...35

Text Alignment in Tables 36

Text Shadow 36

Text Alignment and Accessibility 36

4.5 Using External Stylesheets...36

Benefits of External Stylesheets..37

Creating an External Stylesheet 37

Linking the External Stylesheet to HTML 37

Using the External Stylesheet...38

Benefits of External Stylesheets for Large Projects.......................................38

Chapter 5: Working with Images and Multimedia..39

5.1 Adding Images to Your Web Page..39

The `<img>` Element 39

Relative and Absolute Image Paths 40

Image Accessibility 40

5.2 Image Attributes and Optimization 40

The `src` Attribute 41

The `alt` Attribute 41

The `width` and `height` Attributes..41

Image File Formats 41

Image Compression 42

Responsive Images 42

Lazy Loading 42

Image Accessibility and SEO 42

5.3 Embedding Audio and Video 43

The `<audio>` Element 43

The `<video>` Element 43

Additional Attributes 44

Responsive Media 44

Accessibility 44

5.4 HTML5 Multimedia Elements 45

The `<audio>` Element 45

The `<video>` Element 46

The `<source>` Element 46

The `<canvas>` Element 47

5.5 Responsive Images and Media 47

The Need for Responsive Design 47

Responsive Images 47

Responsive Video 48

Media Queries 49

Testing and Debugging 49

Chapter 6: Hyperlinks and Navigation 50

6.1 Creating Hyperlinks 50

The Anchor Element 50

Linking to Sections within a Page 51

Targeting Links 51

Styling Links with CSS 51

Summary 51

6.2 Relative vs. Absolute URLs 52

Absolute URLs 52

Relative URLs 52

When to Use Absolute vs. Relative URLs 53

Base URL 53

Summary 53

6.3 Linking to Other Pages...54

Relative URLs for Internal Links...54

Absolute URLs for External Links..54

Linking to Email Addresses...54

Opening Links in a New Window or Tab.................................55

Linking to Specific Sections on a Page....................................55

Linking to Files 55

Best Practices for Linking 55

Summary 56

6.4 Navigation Menus and Lists 56

Creating Navigation Menus with Lists....................................56

Styling Navigation Menus with CSS 57

Dropdown Menus 57

Mobile-Friendly Navigation 58

Summary 58

6.5 Styling Links with CSS..58

Basic Link Styles..58

Customizing Link Styles..59

Pseudo-classes and Pseudo-elements 60

Accessibility Considerations..60

Summary 60

Chapter 7: Forms and User Input...61

7.1 Creating HTML Forms..61

The <form> Element..61

Form Controls 61

The name Attribute 62

The <label> Element..62

Submitting Form Data 62

Summary 62

7.2 Form Elements and Attributes..62

Input Types 62

Common Attributes 63

Grouping Form Controls...63

Form Validation..64

Summary 64

7.3 Form Validation 64

    Built-In HTML5 Validation 64

    JavaScript Validation 65

    Summary 66

7.4 Handling Form Submissions 66

    Form Submission Basics 66

    Server-Side Scripting 67

    Validation and Security 67

    Redirecting After Submission 67

    Summary 67

7.5 Advanced Form Features 68

    1. Form Validation with JavaScript 68

    2. Conditional Fields 68

    3. Auto-Suggestions and Auto-Complete 69

    4. Multi-Step Forms 69

    5. File Upload Progress 69

    6. Accessible Forms 69

    Summary 69

Chapter 8: Tables for Data Organization 71

8.1 Creating HTML Tables 71

    Basic Table Structure 71

    Table Headers 71

    Table Borders and Styling 72

    Table Captions 72

    Spanning Rows and Columns 72

    Summary 73

8.2 Table Structure and Elements 73

    Table Sections 73

    Table Headers and Cells 74

    Table Row Grouping 74

    Summary 75

8.3 Styling Tables with CSS 75

    1. Table Borders and Padding 75

2. Table Background Colors 75

3. Text Alignment..76

4. Hover Effects...76

5. Borders and Styling for Specific Columns...76

6. Responsive Tables...76

7. CSS Frameworks 76

8.4 Table Accessibility..77

1. Use Semantic HTML...77

2. Add Table Captions 77

3. Use Header Cells..77

4. Use Scope and Headers Attributes 78

5. Provide Table Summaries 78

6. Test with Screen Readers...78

7. Keyboard Navigation..78

8.5 Responsive Tables 79

1. Horizontal Scrolling...79

2. Hide Columns 79

3. Stack Rows...80

4. Responsive Tables with CSS Frameworks 80

5. Testing on Multiple Devices...80

6. Consider Mobile-First Design...80

Chapter 9: Semantic HTML5 Elements 81

9.1 Understanding Semantic Markup 81

1. The Role of Semantic Elements 81

2. Benefits of Semantic Markup...81

3. Common Semantic Elements 82

4. Using Semantic Elements 82

5. Fallback for Older Browsers 82

9.2 HTML5 Structural Elements..83

1. `<header>` 83

2. `<nav>` 83

3. `<main>` 83

4. `<article>` 84

5. `<section>` 84

6. `<aside>`...84

7. `<footer>`...84

9.3 Using Header and Footer Elements 85

1. The `<header>` Element..85

2. The `<footer>` Element..86

Semantic Benefits 86

9.4 Semantic Tags for Content 86

1. `<article>` 87

2. `<section>` 87

3. `<aside>`..87

4. `<details>` and `<summary>`.............................87

5. `<figure>` and `<figcaption>`.........................88

6. `<mark>` 88

7. `<time>` 88

9.5 ARIA Roles for Accessibility 88

1. `role="banner"`...88

2. `role="navigation"`...89

3. `role="main"` 89

4. `role="complementary"` 89

5. `role="form"` 89

6. `role="button"`...90

7. `aria-label` and `aria-labelledby`.................90

Chapter 10: Multimedia and Embedding...........................91

10.1 Embedding Videos from YouTube 91

1. Obtaining the YouTube Video URL.......................91

2. Embedding with the `<iframe>` Element 91

3. Customizing the Embed Code................................91

4. Responsive Embeds..92

5. JavaScript Integration 92

10.2 Using iFrames for Embedded Content 92

1. Basics of the `<iframe>` Element.......................93

2. Controlling the Size of the `<iframe>` 93

3. Responsive iFrames..93

4. Security Considerations 93

5. Use Cases for `<iframe>` 93

10.3 Creating Interactive Maps 94

1. Embedding Google Maps 94

2. Customizing the Embedded Map 95

3. Responsive Google Maps 95

4. JavaScript Integration 95

10.4 Working with SVG Graphics 96

1. Understanding SVG 96

2. Creating SVG Images 96

3. Basic SVG Elements 96

4. Styling SVG 97

5. Animating SVG 97

6. Accessibility 97

7. Compatibility 97

8. Optimization 97

9. SVG Libraries and Tools 97

10.5 Best Practices for Embedded Media 97

1. Use Standard HTML5 Elements 98

2. Provide Fallback Content 98

3. Implement Accessibility 98

4. Optimize Media 98

5. Ensure Responsiveness 98

6. Consider Lazy Loading 99

7. Test Cross-Browser Compatibility 99

8. Enable Video Autoplay with Caution 99

9. Monitor Performance 99

10. Compliance with Copyright 99

Chapter 11: CSS Basics and Selectors 100

Section 11.1: Introduction to Cascading Style Sheets 100

Why Use CSS? 100

How CSS Works 100

Inline, Internal, and External CSS 101

Section 11.2: CSS Syntax and Declarations 101

CSS Rule Syntax 101

CSS Properties and Values 102

CSS Comments..102

Grouping Selectors 103

Specificity and Cascading 103

Section 11.3: CSS Selectors and Specificity...103

Simple Selectors 104

Combinators..104

Pseudo-classes and Pseudo-elements 105

Specificity 105

Section 11.4: Styling Text and Backgrounds...106

Styling Text...106

Styling Backgrounds 107

Section 11.5: Applying CSS to Multiple Elements 107

Universal Selector...108

Type Selectors 108

Class Selectors 108

ID Selectors...108

Grouping Selectors 109

Pseudo-classes and Pseudo-elements 109

Descendant and Child Selectors 109

Chapter 12: CSS Layout and Positioning 110

Section 12.1: Box Model in CSS...110

Box Model Basics...110

Box Model Properties...110

Example: 110

Section 12.2: CSS Display Properties 111

Block-level and Inline-level Elements...111

Common display Property Values 111

Example: 112

Section 12.3: Positioning Elements..113

The position Property 113

Example: 113

Section 12.4: Floats and Clearing..115

The `float` Property..115

Clearing Floats..115

Example:..115

Section 12.5: Creating Responsive Layouts.......................................116

Media Queries...116

Fluid Grids...117

Flexbox and CSS Grid..117

Mobile-First Design...117

Testing and Debugging..117

Chapter 13: CSS Flexbox and Grid..119

Section 13.1: Understanding Flexbox...119

The Flex Container..119

The Main Axis and Cross Axis...119

Flex Items..119

Section 13.2: Flexbox Properties...120

1. `flex-direction`...120

2. `justify-content`...120

3. `align-items`...121

4. `flex`..121

5. `flex-grow` and `flex-shrink`...121

Section 13.3: Creating Flexbox Layouts...122

1. Simple Horizontal and Vertical Centering...................................122

2. Creating Equal-Width Columns..122

3. Building a Navigation Bar...122

4. Implementing a Sticky Footer...123

5. Responsive Card Layout..123

Section 13.4: Introduction to CSS Grid...123

1. Grid Container and Grid Items..124

2. Defining Grid Rows and Columns...124

3. Placing Grid Items..124

4. Grid Gaps..124

5. Grid Areas...124

6. Responsive Grids..125

7. Browser Support...125

Section 13.5: Grid Layout Examples 125

1. Basic Grid Layout 125

2. Responsive Grid Layout 126

3. Complex Grid Layout..127

4. Grid for Photo Gallery 128

Chapter 14: CSS Transitions and Animations...129

Section 14.1: Transitioning CSS Properties..129

Understanding CSS Transitions 129

Example: Hover Effect 129

Transitioning Multiple Properties..130

Customizing Transition Delays...130

Section 14.2: Keyframe Animations 131

Creating Keyframe Animations...131

Animation Properties..131

Example: Bouncing Ball Animation...132

Keyframe animations are versatile and can be used to create a wide range of
animations, including fading, scaling, rotating, and more. Experiment with different
keyframes and animation properties to bring your web pages to life with engaging and
interactive animations...132

Section 14.3: Creating Smooth Transitions 132

Basics of CSS Transitions...132

Transition Properties...133

Multiple Transitions 133

Transitioning Multiple Properties...134

CSS transitions are a great way to enhance user interactions and provide visual
feedback on web pages. They are particularly useful for creating smooth animations
without the need for complex JavaScript code. Experiment with different transition
properties and timing functions to achieve the desired visual effects in your web
projects...134

Section 14.4: Advanced Animation Techniques 134

1. CSS Animations with Keyframes 134

2. Animation Properties...135

3. JavaScript Animation Libraries..135

4. WebGL and 3D Animations..136

Section 14.5: Browser Compatibility 136

1. CSS Vendor Prefixes..136

2. Browser Testing Tools...137

3. JavaScript Compatibility 137

4. Graceful Degradation and Progressive Enhancement 137

5. Browser-Specific Bugs 137

6. Progressive Enhancement with CSS Animations 137

Chapter 15: Responsive Web Design 139

  Section 15.1: What Is Responsive Web Design?...139

    The Concept of Responsiveness 139

    Key Principles of Responsive Design 139

    Benefits of Responsive Web Design...139

  Section 15.2: Media Queries..140

    Syntax of Media Queries 140

    Using Media Features...140

    Combining Media Features...140

    Mobile-First Approach...141

    Examples of Media Queries..141

  Section 15.3: Fluid Grid Layouts 141

    Understanding Fluid Grids...141

    Using Percentages for Width 142

    Media Queries and Breakpoints 142

    Handling Gutters and Margins 142

    Challenges of Fluid Grids 142

  Section 15.4: Responsive Images..143

    Challenges with Fixed-Size Images 143

    Using `max-width` for Images..143

    The `srcset` Attribute 143

    The `sizes` Attribute...144

    Art Direction with `<picture>`...144

    Conclusion..144

  Section 15.5: Mobile-First Design Approach 144

    The Evolution of Mobile-First..145

    Benefits of Mobile-First Design 145

    How to Implement Mobile-First Design..145

    Conclusion..146

Chapter 16: Cross-Browser Compatibility..147

Section 16.1: Challenges of Cross-Browser Compatibility...147

The Browser Landscape...147

Key Challenges 147

Strategies for Cross-Browser Compatibility 147

Conclusion...148

Section 16.2: Browser Testing Tools...148

1. Browser Developer Tools..148

2. Cross-Browser Testing Platforms...149

3. Browser Extensions and Add-Ons 149

4. Online Testing Tools...149

5. Virtual Machines and Emulators 150

Conclusion...150

Section 16.3: CSS Vendor Prefixes..150

The History of Vendor Prefixes..150

The Problem with Vendor Prefixes...151

The Decline of Vendor Prefixes..151

Best Practices 151

Section 16.4: JavaScript Compatibility 152

Challenges of JavaScript Compatibility..152

Best Practices for JavaScript Compatibility..152

Section 16.5: Graceful Degradation and Progressive Enhancement..........................154

Graceful Degradation 154

Progressive Enhancement 155

Chapter 17: HTML5 and Modern Web Features 157

Section 17.1: HTML5 Features Overview...157

1. Semantic Elements: HTML5 introduced several new semantic elements like
`<header>`, `<nav>`, `<footer>`, and `<article>`. These elements provide a more
meaningful structure to web documents, making it easier for search engines and
assistive technologies to understand the content. 157

2. Audio and Video Support: HTML5 includes native support for embedding audio and
video content using the `<audio>` and `<video>` elements. This eliminates the need for
third-party plugins like Adobe Flash and simplifies multimedia integration. 157

3. Canvas: The `<canvas>` element enables dynamic rendering of graphics and
animations using JavaScript. It has given rise to a wide range of web-based games,
interactive visualizations, and drawing applications..157

4. Local Storage: The Web Storage API, including `localStorage` and `sessionStorage`, allows web applications to store data locally on the user's device. This feature is handy for building offline-capable web apps and caching resources. .157

5. Web Workers: HTML5 introduced web workers, which are background scripts that can run concurrently with the main JavaScript thread. They are often used for tasks that require significant processing power without blocking the user interface...........158

6. Geolocation: With the Geolocation API, web applications can access a user's geographical location. This feature is utilized in various location-based services and mapping applications...158

7. Offline Web Applications: HTML5 introduced the Application Cache (AppCache) API, allowing web apps to work offline. Developers can specify which resources to cache, ensuring that the app remains functional even without an internet connection. 158

Section 17.2: Geolocation and Web Storage...158

Geolocation API 158

Web Storage 159

Section 17.3: Web Workers and APIs 160

Web Workers..160

APIs (Application Programming Interfaces)..161

Section 17.4: Offline Web Applications 162

Service Workers 162

Web Storage 163

Section 17.5: Enhancing User Experience..164

1. Responsive Design...164

2. Performance Optimization..165

3. Usability and Accessibility 165

4. Mobile-First Design...165

5. Clear Navigation and Information Architecture..165

6. Consistency in Design and Branding 165

7. Feedback and Error Handling...166

8. Content Quality 166

9. Mobile App-Like Interactions 166

10. Security and Privacy 166

Chapter 18: Web Accessibility and SEO..167

Section 18.1: Accessibility Standards and Guidelines...167

1. Web Content Accessibility Guidelines (WCAG)...167

2. Section 508 167

3. Americans with Disabilities Act (ADA)......................................167

4. EU Web Accessibility Directive 168

5. Accessible Rich Internet Applications (ARIA) 168

6. Testing and Evaluation Tools 168

7. Inclusive Design..168

8. Benefits of Web Accessibility..168

9. Continuous Improvement 168

Section 18.2: Creating Accessible Content................................168

1. Semantic HTML..169

2. Alternative Text for Images 169

3. Keyboard Navigation..169

4. Focus Styles 169

5. Color Contrast..169

6. Video and Audio Accessibility 170

7. Forms and Error Handling...170

8. Testing with Assistive Technologies......................................170

9. ARIA Roles and Attributes...170

10. Responsive Design 170

11. User Testing...170

Section 18.3: ARIA Roles and Attributes 170

1. ARIA Roles..171

2. ARIA Attributes...171

3. Examples of ARIA Usage 171

4. Testing and Validation 172

Section 18.4: SEO Best Practices 172

1. Keyword Research...173

2. High-Quality Content..173

3. Meta Tags..173

4. Optimize Images and Media 173

5. Internal and External Links...173

6. Mobile-Friendly Design 174

7. Site Speed and Performance 174

8. XML Sitemap and Robots.txt...174

9. Regular Monitoring and Analysis...174

10. Stay Informed...174

Section 18.5: Optimizing for Search Engines..174

  1. Voice Search Optimization..174

  2. Featured Snippets..175

  3. Schema Markup..175

  4. Video SEO...175

  5. Mobile-First Indexing..175

  6. Page Speed Optimization...176

  7. Local SEO...176

  8. Backlink Building..176

  9. User Experience (UX) Optimization...176

  10. Content Freshness...176

Chapter 19: Web Hosting and Deployment..176

  Section 19.1: Choosing a Web Hosting Provider.......................................177

Section 19.2: Uploading Your Website...178

  Uploading Methods...178

  Considerations for Uploading...180

Section 19.3: Domain Name Setup...180

  Domain Name Registration...180

  Domain Name Configuration..181

  SSL Certificate (HTTPS)...182

Section 19.4: SSL Certificates and Security...183

  What is an SSL Certificate?..183

  Why SSL is Important...183

  Obtaining an SSL Certificate...183

  Types of SSL Certificates..183

  Installing an SSL Certificate...184

  Renewing SSL Certificates..184

  Conclusion...184

Section 19.5: Monitoring and Maintenance..185

  The Need for Monitoring and Maintenance..185

  Key Aspects of Website Monitoring and Maintenance.............................185

  Website Maintenance Schedule...186

  Documentation and Tracking...186

Conclusion..186
Chapter 20: Advanced HTML and Beyond..187
Section 20.1: Custom HTML Data Attributes...187
Leveraging Custom Data Attributes 187
  Dynamic Content...187
  Interactive Elements 188
  JavaScript Interaction 188
  Styling with CSS...188
Section 20.2: Microdata and Schema.org 188
  Understanding Microdata 188
  Benefits of Microdata 189
  Using Schema.org..189
  Integrating Microdata 190
Section 20.3: Web Components...190
  Custom Elements 190
  Shadow DOM..190
  HTML Templates..191
Section 20.4: WebAssembly and HTML Future 192
  How WebAssembly Works 192
  The Future of HTML 193
Section 20.5: Staying Updated in the HTML World 193

Chapter 1: Introduction to HTML

1.1 What is HTML?

HTML (Hypertext Markup Language) is a standard markup language used to create and structure content on the World Wide Web. It serves as the foundation for web pages and defines the structure and semantics of the content. HTML documents consist of elements and tags that instruct web browsers on how to display text, images, links, forms, and other media.

HTML is not a programming language; instead, it's a markup language. This means that HTML documents are created using a set of predefined tags and attributes, which describe the elements within a web page. These elements can include headings, paragraphs, lists, images, hyperlinks, and more.

HTML Basics

At its core, HTML consists of opening and closing tags that enclose content. For example, to create a paragraph of text, you would use the <p> tag:

```
<p>This is a paragraph of text.</p>
```

Here, <p> is the opening tag, and </p> is the closing tag. The content "This is a paragraph of text." is placed between these tags and will be displayed as a paragraph on the web page.

Structure of an HTML Document

An HTML document typically consists of several sections, including the <html>, <head>, and <body> elements. Here's a basic structure:

```
<!DOCTYPE html>
<html>
  <head>
    <title>Page Title</title>
  </head>
  <body>
    <h1>Heading 1</h1>
    <p>This is a paragraph of text.</p>
    <img src="image.jpg" alt="An image" />
    <a href="https://www.example.com">Visit Example.com</a>
  </body>
</html>
```

- <!DOCTYPE html>: Declares the document as an HTML5 document.
- <html>: The root element that encloses the entire document.
- <head>: Contains metadata about the document, such as the title.
- <body>: Contains the visible content of the web page, including headings, paragraphs, images, and links.

Semantic HTML

HTML also introduces semantic elements like `<header>`, `<nav>`, `<article>`, `<footer>`, and more. These elements provide meaning to the structure of the content and are essential for accessibility and SEO (Search Engine Optimization).

HTML has evolved over the years, and HTML5 is the latest version, offering new elements and features to enhance web page development.

In summary, HTML is the backbone of web development, providing the essential markup for creating web pages and defining their structure and content.

Feel free to explore the subsequent sections of this chapter to learn more about the history of HTML, its differences from XHTML, and the tools used for HTML development.

1.2 The History of HTML

The history of HTML is a journey that spans several decades and has witnessed significant developments in the world of web technology. Understanding this history provides valuable context for web developers and designers.

HTML in the Early Days

HTML was first proposed by Tim Berners-Lee in 1989 as a means to share documents among researchers at CERN (European Organization for Nuclear Research). The initial version, HTML 1.0, was relatively simple, primarily focused on structuring text and creating hyperlinks.

HTML 2.0, released in 1995, introduced more features, including forms and tables, which allowed for greater interactivity and layout control. This version laid the foundation for the rapid growth of the World Wide Web.

The Browser Wars and HTML 3.2

The mid-'90s saw the "browser wars" between Netscape Navigator and Microsoft Internet Explorer. This competition led to the development of new HTML features and tags, resulting in HTML 3.2. This version added support for frames, which enabled multiple documents to be displayed within a single web page.

HTML 4.01 and XHTML

HTML 4.01, released in 1999, introduced stricter rules for document structure and improved support for style sheets. It marked a significant step towards standardization.

XHTML (Extensible Hypertext Markup Language) emerged as a reformulation of HTML as an XML application. XHTML 1.0 and 1.1, which followed HTML 4.01, enforced stricter syntax rules and aimed for greater compatibility with XML.

HTML5, officially released in 2014, represented a major milestone in web development. It introduced a plethora of new elements and features, making it possible to create rich, interactive web applications without relying heavily on plugins like Flash. HTML5's native video and audio support, canvas for graphics, and improved forms capabilities revolutionized web development.

Ongoing Evolution

HTML continues to evolve, with ongoing updates and refinements. The development community, web standards organizations, and browser vendors collaborate to define and implement new features.

Web developers should keep up with the latest HTML specifications and best practices to create modern, accessible, and efficient web experiences.

In summary, the history of HTML reflects the dynamic nature of the web. From its humble beginnings as a simple markup language, HTML has evolved into a powerful tool for creating diverse and interactive web content. Understanding this history is crucial for staying current in web development.

1.3 HTML vs. XHTML

HTML and XHTML are two related but distinct markup languages used for web development. Understanding their differences is essential for web developers, as it can impact how web pages are constructed and rendered by browsers.

HTML (Hypertext Markup Language)

HTML, or Hypertext Markup Language, is the standard markup language used for creating web pages. It is designed to be both human-readable and machine-readable. HTML documents can be more forgiving of syntax errors, making it suitable for web pages with varying levels of complexity.

In HTML, tags do not necessarily need to be closed, but it is common practice to close them for clarity. For example, an HTML paragraph tag can be written as <p> or <p></p>. HTML allows for some flexibility in attribute values and case sensitivity.

XHTML (Extensible Hypertext Markup Language)

XHTML, or Extensible Hypertext Markup Language, is a stricter and more XML-like version of HTML. It is designed to be more consistent, well-formed, and adhere to XML standards. XHTML requires all tags to be properly closed and follow a well-defined structure. This means that every opening tag must have a corresponding closing tag.

For example, in XHTML, a paragraph tag must always be written as `<p></p>`. Additionally, attribute values in XHTML must always be enclosed in double quotes, and tag and attribute names must be in lowercase.

```
<!-- XHTML Example -->
<p class="important">This is a paragraph.</p>
```

1. **Syntax Rules**: The most significant difference between HTML and XHTML is the syntax. XHTML has stricter rules, enforces well-formedness, and requires all tags to be properly closed.

2. **Case Sensitivity**: XHTML is case-sensitive, meaning that tag and attribute names must be in lowercase.

3. **Attribute Values**: In XHTML, attribute values must always be enclosed in double quotes, while HTML is more lenient in this regard.

4. **Self-Closing Tags**: XHTML mandates that self-closing tags (e.g., `<img />`, `<br />`) include the trailing slash, while HTML often omits it.

5. **DOCTYPE Declaration**: XHTML documents require a specific DOCTYPE declaration, such as `<!DOCTYPE html>`, to be considered valid.

Choosing Between HTML and XHTML

The choice between HTML and XHTML depends on the project's requirements and personal preferences. HTML is generally more forgiving and suitable for simpler web pages, while XHTML's stricter syntax is preferred for projects where adherence to standards and compatibility with XML tools are crucial.

Web developers should be aware of these differences and select the markup language that aligns with the project's goals and best practices. Additionally, modern web development often emphasizes the use of HTML5, which combines HTML's familiarity with some of XHTML's stricter rules, making it a popular choice for contemporary web development.

1.4 Anatomy of an HTML Document

To effectively work with HTML, it's crucial to understand the structure and components of an HTML document. An HTML document is essentially a text file that contains markup instructions for web browsers to interpret and display content. Let's break down the essential components of an HTML document:

Document Type Declaration

Every HTML document begins with a Document Type Declaration (DOCTYPE). This declaration tells the browser which version of HTML (or XHTML) the document adheres to. For HTML5, the DOCTYPE declaration is as follows:

```
<!DOCTYPE html>
```

HTML Element

The root element of an HTML document is `<html>`. It wraps all the content on the page and defines the document type as HTML5.

```
<!DOCTYPE html>
<html>
  <!-- Content goes here -->
</html>
```

Head Section

Inside the `<html>` element, you'll find the `<head>` section. This section contains metadata and information about the document, but it doesn't display directly on the web page. Common elements within the `<head>` section include:

- `<title>`: Sets the title of the web page, displayed in the browser's title bar or tab.
- `<meta>`: Provides metadata about the document, such as character encoding and viewport settings.
- `<link>`: Links to external resources like stylesheets or icon files.
- `<script>`: Includes JavaScript code that can affect the behavior and functionality of the web page.

```
<!DOCTYPE html>
<html>
  <head>
    <meta charset="UTF-8">
    <title>My Web Page</title>
    <link rel="stylesheet" href="styles.css">
    <script src="script.js"></script>
  </head>
  <!-- Content goes here -->
</html>
```

Body Section

The `<body>` section contains the visible content of the web page, such as text, images, links, and multimedia elements. This is where you structure your web page and create the user interface.

```
<!DOCTYPE html>
<html>
  <head>
    <!-- Metadata -->
  </head>
  <body>
    <header>
      <h1>Welcome to My Web Page</h1>
    </header>
```

```
<nav>
  <ul>
    <li><a href="/">Home</a></li>
    <li><a href="/about">About</a></li>
    <li><a href="/contact">Contact</a></li>
  </ul>
</nav>
<main>
  <p>This is the main content of the page.</p>
  <img src="image.jpg" alt="An image">
</main>
<footer>
  &copy; 2023 My Website
</footer>
</body>
</html>
```

Comments

You can add comments to your HTML code to provide explanations or annotations. HTML comments are enclosed in `<!--` and `-->`. They are not displayed on the web page and are solely for the developer's reference.

```
<!-- This is a comment -->
```

Understanding the anatomy of an HTML document is the foundation for creating well-structured and semantically meaningful web pages. By organizing your content within these elements, you can create web pages that are both functional and user-friendly.

1.5 Tools for HTML Development

When working with HTML, having the right set of tools can significantly enhance your development workflow and productivity. Whether you're a beginner or an experienced web developer, here are some essential tools for HTML development:

1. Text Editors

A good text editor is the foundation of web development. There are many text editors available, both free and paid, that are well-suited for HTML development. Some popular choices include:

- **Visual Studio Code (VS Code)**: A free, open-source code editor by Microsoft, known for its rich ecosystem of extensions and excellent HTML support.

- **Sublime Text**: A lightweight and highly customizable text editor with a vibrant community of users and plugins.

- **Atom**: Another free and open-source text editor developed by GitHub, known for its ease of use and extensibility.

- **Brackets**: An open-source text editor designed specifically for web development, with features like live preview and preprocessor support.

2. Integrated Development Environments (IDEs)

Integrated Development Environments provide more than just a text editor; they often include features like code completion, debugging tools, and project management. Some popular HTML-focused IDEs include:

- **WebStorm**: A commercial IDE by JetBrains that offers comprehensive web development support, including HTML, CSS, and JavaScript.

- **Eclipse**: An open-source IDE that can be extended with web development plugins for HTML, CSS, and JavaScript.

- **NetBeans**: A free, open-source IDE that supports web development and offers features like code templates and project management.

3. Browsers and Developer Tools

Browsers are essential for testing your HTML code and ensuring it displays correctly. Most modern browsers come with built-in developer tools that allow you to inspect HTML elements, CSS styles, and debug JavaScript. Some popular browsers for web development include:

- **Google Chrome**: Known for its robust developer tools, Chrome is a favorite among web developers for debugging and performance testing.

- **Mozilla Firefox**: Firefox offers a powerful set of developer tools and is often used for web development and debugging.

- **Microsoft Edge**: The Chromium-based version of Microsoft Edge provides a similar developer experience to Google Chrome.

4. Version Control Systems

Version control systems (VCS) are crucial for tracking changes to your HTML code, collaborating with others, and rolling back to previous versions if needed. Popular VCS options include Git (with platforms like GitHub and GitLab) and Subversion.

5. Package Managers

Package managers like npm (Node Package Manager) and yarn help manage and install third-party libraries and frameworks, including those related to HTML development.

6. Code Validators

Online validators and linters can check your HTML code for syntax errors and adherence to best practices. The W3C Markup Validation Service is a popular choice for HTML validation.

7. Code Editors for Collaboration

For collaborative coding sessions, tools like Visual Studio Live Share or Google Docs can help multiple developers work together in real-time on the same HTML document.

8. Frameworks and Libraries

Depending on your project's complexity, you may find it beneficial to use HTML frameworks and libraries. These can streamline development and provide pre-built components and styles. Popular choices include Bootstrap, Foundation, and Materialize for CSS, as well as jQuery for JavaScript interaction.

9. Web Hosting and Deployment Services

When you're ready to publish your HTML-based website, web hosting services like Netlify, GitHub Pages, or traditional hosting providers can help you deploy your code to the web.

These tools and resources can greatly enhance your HTML development workflow, making it easier to create, test, and maintain web pages and applications. Depending on your specific needs and preferences, you can choose the tools that best fit your development style.

Chapter 2: Setting Up Your HTML Environment

2.1 Choosing a Text Editor

Choosing the right text editor is one of the first decisions you'll make when setting up your HTML development environment. Your choice of text editor can significantly impact your productivity and coding experience. Here are some considerations and popular text editors to help you make an informed decision:

Considerations for Choosing a Text Editor

1. **Ease of Use**: An intuitive and user-friendly interface is essential for a smooth coding experience. You want a text editor that makes it easy to write and manage HTML code.

2. **Cross-Platform Compatibility**: Depending on your operating system (Windows, macOS, Linux), you'll want a text editor that is available and functions well on your platform of choice.

3. **Customization**: The ability to customize the text editor's appearance and functionality can be a big plus. Many text editors support themes, extensions, and plugins that allow you to tailor the environment to your preferences.

4. **Code Highlighting**: Syntax highlighting is crucial for quickly identifying HTML elements, tags, and attributes. Look for a text editor that provides robust code highlighting.

5. **Autocompletion**: Autocompletion or code suggestions can save you time by automatically completing tags and attributes as you type.

6. **Integration**: Some text editors integrate seamlessly with version control systems, build tools, and web development frameworks, streamlining your workflow.

7. **Performance**: A responsive and fast text editor is essential for an efficient coding experience, especially when working on large HTML projects.

Popular Text Editors for HTML Development

1. **Visual Studio Code (VS Code)**: A highly popular and free text editor developed by Microsoft. It offers a wide range of extensions, excellent HTML support, and a vibrant community.

2. **Sublime Text**: Known for its speed and minimalistic design, Sublime Text is a favorite among developers. It supports HTML syntax highlighting and offers a wide array of plugins.

3. **Atom**: An open-source and customizable text editor by GitHub. Atom is known for its user-friendly interface and extensive package ecosystem.

4. **Brackets**: Specifically designed for web development, Brackets offers live preview features and integrates seamlessly with HTML, CSS, and JavaScript.

5. **Notepad++**: A free and open-source text editor for Windows users. While not as feature-rich as some others, it's lightweight and gets the job done.

6. **TextMate**: A macOS text editor known for its simplicity and powerful bundle system for extending functionality.

7. **Vim**: A highly configurable and efficient text editor, Vim is a favorite among developers who prefer keyboard shortcuts and a terminal-based interface.

Ultimately, the best text editor for HTML development depends on your preferences and needs. You may want to try a few different options to see which one aligns best with your workflow and coding style. Additionally, many of these text editors are highly extensible, allowing you to tailor them to your specific requirements as your HTML skills progress.

2.2 Installing a Web Browser

A web browser is a fundamental tool for web development, as it allows you to view and test the HTML, CSS, and JavaScript code you write. Most operating systems come with a default web browser pre-installed, but it's a good practice to have multiple browsers available for testing, as different browsers may interpret code slightly differently. In this section, we'll discuss how to install and set up web browsers for web development.

Default Web Browsers

1. **Google Chrome**: Google Chrome is one of the most popular web browsers, known for its developer tools and extensive extension ecosystem. It's available for Windows, macOS, and Linux. You can download it from the Google Chrome website.

2. **Mozilla Firefox**: Firefox is another widely used browser with robust developer tools. It's available for multiple platforms, including Windows, macOS, and Linux. You can download it from the Mozilla Firefox website.

3. **Microsoft Edge**: Microsoft Edge, based on the Chromium engine, is available for Windows and macOS. It's notable for its integration with Windows and developer tools. It comes pre-installed on Windows but can also be downloaded for macOS from the Microsoft Edge website.

Browser Testing

To ensure that your web pages work correctly across different browsers, you should test them in various browsers. Here are some tips for effective browser testing:

1. **Multiple Browsers**: Install and use multiple browsers for testing. Google Chrome, Mozilla Firefox, and Microsoft Edge are good choices.

2. **Browser Dev Tools**: Familiarize yourself with each browser's developer tools. These tools allow you to inspect elements, view console logs, and debug JavaScript.

3. **Responsive Design**: Test your web pages on different screen sizes by using the responsive design mode available in browser developer tools.

4. **Browser Extensions**: Consider using browser extensions like the "Web Developer" extension for Firefox and Chrome, which adds additional development tools to your browser.

5. **Online Services**: Explore online services like BrowserStack and CrossBrowserTesting, which provide access to multiple browsers and platforms for testing.

Mobile Browsers

In addition to desktop browsers, it's essential to test your web pages on mobile devices. Most modern browsers come with mobile emulation features in their developer tools, allowing you to simulate how your site will appear and function on smartphones and tablets. You can also use physical devices or mobile testing platforms like BrowserStack for thorough mobile testing.

Keeping Browsers Updated

Web browsers regularly receive updates to improve performance, security, and web standards support. It's essential to keep your browsers up to date to ensure accurate testing and compatibility with the latest web technologies.

By having a selection of browsers and keeping them up to date, you'll be better equipped to create web pages and applications that work seamlessly across different environments, enhancing the user experience for all visitors.

2.3 Setting Up a Local Development Server

When developing HTML projects, it's common to work on your local computer before deploying your web pages to a live server. To do this effectively, you'll need a local development server. A local server allows you to run your HTML files and test them in a web browser, simulating how they will behave when hosted on a remote server. In this section, we'll explore how to set up a local development server.

Why Use a Local Development Server?

Using a local development server provides several benefits:

1. **Simulated Environment**: It simulates a web server environment on your computer, allowing you to test your HTML, CSS, and JavaScript files locally before deploying them to a live server.

2. **No Internet Required**: You can work on your projects without an internet connection, which is especially useful when developing in remote locations or during internet outages.

3. **Faster Testing**: Local servers typically serve files faster than remote servers, reducing the time it takes to preview changes.

4. **Isolated Testing**: Your local server environment is isolated from the internet, providing a secure space for testing without affecting your live websites.

Setting Up a Local Development Server

1. Using Python's SimpleHTTPServer (Python 2) or http.server (Python 3)

If you have Python installed on your computer, you can use its built-in HTTP server to quickly set up a local server. Here are the steps:

For Python 2 (SimpleHTTPServer):

Open your terminal or command prompt, navigate to the directory where your HTML files are located, and run the following command:

```
python -m SimpleHTTPServer
```

This starts a local server on port 8000. You can access your files by opening a web browser and navigating to `http://localhost:8000`.

For Python 3 (http.server):

Open your terminal or command prompt, navigate to the directory where your HTML files are located, and run the following command:

```
python -m http.server
```

This starts a local server on port 8000. You can access your files by opening a web browser and navigating to `http://localhost:8000`.

2. Using Node.js and the http-server Package

Node.js is a JavaScript runtime that allows you to run JavaScript on the server side. You can use Node.js and the `http-server` package to set up a local server:

1. If you don't have Node.js installed, download and install it from the official Node.js website.

2. Open your terminal or command prompt, navigate to the directory where your HTML files are located, and run the following commands:

```
# Install the http-server package globally (you only need to do this once)
npm install -g http-server
```

```
# Start the local server
http-server
```

This starts a local server on port 8080 by default. You can access your files by opening a web browser and navigating to `http://localhost:8080`.

3. Using Visual Studio Code

If you're using Visual Studio Code (VS Code) as your text editor, it has a built-in feature for running a local server. Here's how to use it:

1. Open your project folder in VS Code.

2. Open the HTML file you want to preview.

3. Right-click on the HTML file's tab and select "Open with Live Server."

This will start a local server and open your HTML file in a web browser.

4. Other Local Server Options

There are also standalone local server applications like XAMPP, WampServer (for Windows), and MAMP (for macOS) that provide a full web server environment for local development. These tools can be useful for more complex projects or when you need to work with server-side scripting languages like PHP.

Using a Local Development Server

Once you've set up your local development server, you can use it to:

- Preview your HTML files in a web browser by accessing `http://localhost:{port}`.
- Test your web pages and interact with them as if they were hosted on a remote server.
- Debug and troubleshoot any issues before deploying your projects to a live server.

Local development servers are invaluable tools for web developers, as they provide a safe and efficient way to work on web projects before making them accessible to the world.

2.4 Creating Your First HTML Document

Now that you have set up your local development environment, it's time to create your first HTML document. This document will serve as the foundation for your web page and is essential for understanding the structure of an HTML file. In this section, we'll walk through the steps to create a basic HTML document.

Step 1: Open a Text Editor

Open your chosen text editor (e.g., Visual Studio Code, Sublime Text, or any text editor you prefer). You should see a blank canvas where you can start typing your HTML code.

An HTML document follows a specific structure. It begins with a `<!DOCTYPE>` declaration, followed by an `<html>` element that contains a `<head>` section and a `<body>` section. Here's a breakdown:

- `<!DOCTYPE html>`: This declaration specifies that you are using HTML5, the latest version of HTML.

- `<html>`: This element is the root of your HTML document and contains all other elements.

- `<head>`: Inside the `<html>` element, the `<head>` section contains metadata about your document, such as the page title and character encoding.

- `<body>`: The `<body>` section contains the visible content of your web page, including text, images, links, and more.

Here's an example of this basic structure:

```
<!DOCTYPE html>
<html>
  <head>
    <meta charset="UTF-8">
    <title>My First Web Page</title>
  </head>
  <body>
    <h1>Welcome to My Web Page</h1>
    <p>This is my first HTML document.</p>
  </body>
</html>
```

Step 3: Add Content

Inside the `<body>` section, you can add content to your web page. HTML provides various elements for structuring and formatting content. In the example above, we've used the following elements:

- `<h1>`: This is a heading element, and it represents the main heading of the page.

- `<p>`: This is a paragraph element, used for regular text.

You can expand your web page by adding more elements like headings, paragraphs, lists, links, and images. Experiment with different elements to structure your content as needed.

Step 4: Save Your HTML File

Once you've added content, save your file with an `.html` extension. Choose a meaningful filename, such as `index.html`. Ensure that your text editor is set to save the file as plain text or HTML.

To view your web page, open your web browser and navigate to `http://localhost:{port}/{path}`, where {port} is the port number of your local development server, and {path} is the path to your HTML file relative to the server's root directory. For example, if you saved your file as `index.html` and your server is running on port 8080, you would visit `http://localhost:8080/index.html`.

You should see your web page displayed in the browser, showing the content you added.

Congratulations! You've created your first HTML document. This is the starting point for building more complex web pages and applications. As you continue your HTML journey, you'll learn about additional HTML elements, styling with CSS, and adding interactivity with JavaScript to create dynamic and engaging web experiences.

2.5 Validating Your HTML Code

After creating your HTML documents, it's essential to ensure that your code is well-formed and follows HTML standards. HTML validation is the process of checking your code against the official HTML specifications to identify any errors or inconsistencies. Valid HTML code is more likely to display correctly across different browsers and devices, enhancing the user experience. In this section, we'll explore the importance of HTML validation and how to validate your code.

Why HTML Validation Matters

1. **Cross-Browser Compatibility**: Valid HTML code is more likely to render consistently across various web browsers, reducing the chance of layout and functionality issues.

2. **Accessibility**: Valid HTML is a foundation for creating accessible websites that can be used by individuals with disabilities. Properly structured HTML can be interpreted by assistive technologies like screen readers.

3. **Search Engine Optimization (SEO)**: Search engines use well-structured HTML to understand and index web content effectively. Valid HTML can contribute to better SEO rankings.

4. **Future-Proofing**: Adhering to HTML standards ensures that your code will remain compatible with future web technologies and standards.

How to Validate HTML Code

There are several ways to validate your HTML code:

1. Online Validators

Online HTML validators are user-friendly tools that check your HTML code for errors and provide detailed reports. The W3C Markup Validation Service is one of the most widely used online validators. Here's how to use it:

- Go to the W3C Markup Validation Service.

- Enter the URL of your web page or upload your HTML file.

- Click the "Check" or "Validate" button.

- The validator will analyze your HTML code and provide a report indicating any errors or warnings found.

2. Browser Developer Tools

Modern web browsers come equipped with developer tools that include HTML validation. Here's how to use it:

- Open the web page you want to validate in your browser.

- Right-click on the page and select "Inspect" or press `Ctrl + Shift + I` (Windows/Linux) or `Cmd + Option + I` (macOS) to open the developer tools.

- In the developer tools panel, go to the "Console" or "Console/Errors" tab.

- Any HTML validation errors or warnings will be displayed in the console.

3. Integrated Development Environments (IDEs)

Some integrated development environments, such as Visual Studio Code, offer extensions that can check your HTML code for errors as you type. These extensions provide real-time feedback and can help you catch mistakes early in the development process.

4. Command-Line Tools

If you prefer a command-line approach, you can use tools like `html-validator-cli` to validate your HTML files. These tools can be especially useful in automated testing and build pipelines.

Interpreting Validation Results

When you validate your HTML code, you may encounter various types of results:

- **Errors**: These are issues that must be addressed, as they violate HTML standards and can lead to rendering or functionality problems. Common errors include unclosed tags and incorrect attribute values.

- **Warnings**: Warnings indicate potential issues that may not break your page but could affect how it's displayed or interpreted. It's a good practice to review and address warnings whenever possible.

- **Informational Messages**: These messages provide additional information about your HTML code but are not typically associated with errors or warnings.

Fixing Validation Issues

To address validation issues in your HTML code, follow these steps:

1. Review the validation report to identify the specific errors or warnings.

2. Locate the corresponding lines of code in your HTML document.

3. Make the necessary corrections based on the error or warning messages.

4. Revalidate your HTML code to ensure that all issues have been resolved.

By regularly validating your HTML code and addressing any issues that arise, you can create web pages that adhere to standards, provide a better user experience, and perform well across different browsers and devices.

Chapter 3: Basic HTML Structure

3.1 HTML Document Structure

Understanding the structure of an HTML document is fundamental to web development. HTML (Hypertext Markup Language) is the standard language used to create web pages. In this section, we'll delve into the basic structure of an HTML document and learn how to create well-formed HTML code.

The Anatomy of an HTML Element

HTML documents are built using a combination of elements. An element consists of an opening tag, content, and a closing tag. The opening tag defines the beginning of an element, while the closing tag marks the end. Here's a simple example:

```
<p>This is a paragraph.</p>
```

In this example:

- `<p>` is the opening tag.
- `This is a paragraph.` is the content.
- `</p>` is the closing tag.

HTML elements can be nested within each other to create a hierarchy. For example, you can place a paragraph (`<p>`) element inside a division (`<div>`) element:

```
<div>
  <p>This is a paragraph inside a div.</p>
</div>
```

The Basic Structure of an HTML Document

An HTML document has a specific structure that includes the following key elements:

1. `<!DOCTYPE html>`: This declaration, called a DOCTYPE declaration, specifies the version of HTML you are using. In modern web development, `<!DOCTYPE html>` indicates that you are using HTML5, the latest version of HTML.

2. `<html>`: The `<html>` element is the root of the HTML document and contains all other elements.

3. `<head>`: Inside the `<html>` element, the `<head>` section contains metadata about the document, such as the page title, character encoding, and links to external resources.

4. `<title>`: The `<title>` element, located within the `<head>` section, sets the title of the web page, which is displayed in the browser's title bar or tab.

5. `<meta charset="UTF-8">`: This `<meta>` element, also in the `<head>` section, specifies the character encoding for the document. UTF-8 is a widely used encoding that supports a broad range of characters and languages.

6. `<body>`: The `<body>` section contains the visible content of the web page, including text, images, links, and multimedia elements.

Here is an example of a complete HTML document structure:

```
<!DOCTYPE html>
<html>
  <head>
    <meta charset="UTF-8">
    <title>My First Web Page</title>
  </head>
  <body>
    <h1>Welcome to My Web Page</h1>
    <p>This is the main content of the page.</p>
  </body>
</html>
```

This basic structure forms the foundation of all HTML documents. Understanding how to organize your content within this structure is essential for creating well-structured and semantically meaningful web pages. In the following sections, we'll explore various HTML elements and their uses in more detail.

3.2 HTML Elements and Tags

HTML (Hypertext Markup Language) uses a variety of elements and tags to define the structure and content of a web page. Elements are the building blocks of HTML documents, and they are denoted by opening and closing tags. Understanding these elements is crucial for creating web content. In this section, we'll explore some of the most commonly used HTML elements and tags.

1. Headings (`<h1>` to `<h6>`)

Headings are used to define the hierarchy and structure of your content. There are six levels of headings, `<h1>` being the highest and most important, and `<h6>` being the lowest. Here's an example:

```
<h1>This is a level 1 heading</h1>
<h2>This is a level 2 heading</h2>
<h3>This is a level 3 heading</h3>
<h4>This is a level 4 heading</h4>
<h5>This is a level 5 heading</h5>
<h6>This is a level 6 heading</h6>
```

2. Paragraphs (`<p>`)

The `<p>` element is used to create paragraphs of text. It is one of the most common elements for structuring text content on a web page:

```
<p>This is a paragraph of text. It can contain multiple sentences.</p>
```

3. Links (`<a>`)

Links are used to navigate between web pages or resources. The `<a>` element (anchor) is used to create hyperlinks. You specify the destination URL using the `href` attribute:

```
<a href="https://www.example.com">Visit Example.com</a>
```

4. Lists (`<ul>`, `<ol>`, and `<li>`)

HTML supports ordered lists (`<ol>`) and unordered lists (`<ul>`) for organizing items. Each list item is defined with the `<li>` element:

```
<ul>
   <li>Item 1</li>
   <li>Item 2</li>
   <li>Item 3</li>
</ul>

<ol>
   <li>First</li>
   <li>Second</li>
   <li>Third</li>
</ol>
```

5. Images (`<img>`)

To display images on a web page, you use the `<img>` element. It requires the `src` attribute to specify the image file's source (URL or local path):

```
<img src="image.jpg" alt="A beautiful sunset">
```

6. Links to Local Resources (`<a>` with href)

Links can also point to local resources within the same website. For these links, you specify a relative path:

```
<a href="/about.html">About Us</a>
```

7. Line Breaks (`<br>`)

The `<br>` element is used to insert line breaks within text or content. It does not require a closing tag:

```
<p>This is a line of text.<br>Here is the next line.</p>
```

8. Horizontal Lines (`<hr>`)

The `<hr>` element is used to create a horizontal line or thematic break within content:

```
<p>Content above the line.</p>
<hr>
<p>Content below the line.</p>
```

9. Comments (`<!-- -->`)

You can add comments to your HTML code using the `<!--` and `-->` delimiters. Comments are not visible in the rendered web page and are useful for adding notes or explanations:

```
<!-- This is a comment. -->
```

These are just a few examples of HTML elements and tags. HTML provides a wide range of elements for structuring and presenting content, and you can combine them to create rich and interactive web pages. Understanding how to use these elements effectively is essential for web development.

3.3 Headings and Paragraphs

Headings and paragraphs are fundamental elements for structuring text content on a web page. In HTML, headings are represented by `<h1>` to `<h6>` elements, while paragraphs are represented by the `<p>` element. These elements play a crucial role in organizing and presenting textual information. In this section, we'll explore how to use headings and paragraphs effectively.

Headings (`<h1>` to `<h6>`)

HTML provides six levels of headings, from `<h1>` (the highest level) to `<h6>` (the lowest level). Headings are used to define the hierarchical structure of your content, with `<h1>` indicating the main heading and `<h6>` representing the lowest-level subheading. Here's a breakdown of how to use headings:

```
<h1>This is a level 1 heading</h1>
<h2>This is a level 2 heading</h2>
<h3>This is a level 3 heading</h3>
<h4>This is a level 4 heading</h4>
<h5>This is a level 5 heading</h5>
<h6>This is a level 6 heading</h6>
```

When creating a web page, it's essential to use headings in a logical and meaningful way. The main heading (`<h1>`) should represent the primary topic or title of the page, while subheadings (`<h2>`, `<h3>`, etc.) should be used to organize content hierarchically.

Search engines and assistive technologies use heading elements to understand the structure of a page and present it to users. Properly structured headings improve the accessibility and SEO (Search Engine Optimization) of your web content.

Paragraphs (<p>)

The <p> element is used to create paragraphs of text. It represents a block of text and is one of the most common HTML elements for structuring textual content:

```
<p>This is a paragraph of text. It can contain multiple sentences and line breaks.</p>
```

You can use multiple <p> elements to separate and structure different paragraphs within your content.

Combining Headings and Paragraphs

In practice, web pages often combine headings and paragraphs to present information in a clear and organized manner. For example, you might use a top-level heading to introduce a section and follow it with paragraphs that provide details:

```
<h2>About Us</h2>
<p>Welcome to our website. We are a passionate team of individuals...</p>
<p>Our mission is to provide high-quality products and services...</p>
```

Using headings and paragraphs appropriately enhances the readability and comprehension of your web content. It also helps users and search engines quickly grasp the main topics and subtopics of a page.

Styling Headings and Paragraphs with CSS

While HTML defines the structure of headings and paragraphs, you can apply CSS (Cascading Style Sheets) to control their appearance. CSS allows you to change font styles, colors, spacing, and more. By combining HTML and CSS, you can achieve a wide range of design effects to suit your web page's aesthetics and branding.

For example, you can change the color and font size of headings like this:

```
<h1 style="color: #0078d4; font-size: 24px;">Welcome to Our Website</h1>
```

However, it's generally considered best practice to separate content (HTML) from presentation (CSS). To do this, you can define CSS styles in a separate stylesheet and apply them to your HTML elements using classes or IDs.

In summary, headings and paragraphs are essential building blocks for structuring and presenting textual content on a web page. Properly using these elements, along with CSS for styling, improves the readability, accessibility, and visual appeal of your web content.

3.4 Lists and Links

Lists and links are essential elements in HTML that allow you to organize and navigate content effectively. In this section, we'll explore two primary types of lists: ordered lists (<ol>) and unordered lists (<ul>). Additionally, we'll delve into hyperlinks (<a>) and how to create links to different pages and resources.

Ordered Lists (<ol>) and List Items (<li>)

An ordered list (<ol>) is used to present items in a sequential or numbered order. Each list item is represented by the <li> element. Here's an example of an ordered list:

```
<ol>
  <li>First item</li>
  <li>Second item</li>
  <li>Third item</li>
</ol>
```

The above code will render as:

1. First item
2. Second item
3. Third item

You can nest ordered lists within each other to create sublists, maintaining the numbering sequence:

```
<ol>
  <li>First item</li>
  <li>Second item
    <ol>
      <li>Nested item 1</li>
      <li>Nested item 2</li>
    </ol>
  </li>
  <li>Third item</li>
</ol>
```

This will produce:

1. First item
2. Second item
    1. Nested item 1
    2. Nested item 2
3. Third item

Unordered Lists (`<ul>`) and List Items (`<li>`)

An unordered list (`<ul>`) is used to present items in a bulleted or unordered fashion. Like ordered lists, each list item is represented by the `<li>` element:

```
<ul>
   <li>Item A</li>
   <li>Item B</li>
   <li>Item C</li>
</ul>
```

The above code will render as:

- Item A
- Item B
- Item C

Unordered lists are commonly used when the order of items doesn't matter, such as lists of features, benefits, or options.

Hyperlinks (`<a>`)

Hyperlinks, created using the `<a>` (anchor) element, allow you to navigate between web pages or link to external resources. To create a hyperlink, you specify the destination URL using the `href` attribute:

```
<a href="https://www.example.com">Visit Example.com</a>
```

The text between the opening and closing `<a>` tags becomes the clickable link text:

- Visit Example.com

Linking to Local Resources

In addition to linking to external websites, you can create links to other pages within your website by specifying a relative URL:

```
<a href="/about.html">About Us</a>
```

Here, `/about.html` is a relative URL that points to the "about.html" page in the root directory of the website. Relative URLs are a common way to link between pages within the same site.

Linking to Email Addresses

You can also create links that allow users to send emails by specifying an email address in the `href` attribute with the "mailto:" protocol:

```
<a href="mailto:info@example.com">Contact Us</a>
```

When a user clicks this link, it opens their default email client with the recipient address pre-filled.

Linking to Specific Sections of a Page

HTML allows you to create links that navigate to specific sections within a single web page. This is achieved by using IDs and anchor tags. First, you assign an ID to the target section:

```
<h2 id="section1">Section 1</h2>
```

Then, you create a link that points to that ID:

```
<a href="#section1">Go to Section 1</a>
```

When users click the link, the page scrolls to the specified section.

In summary, lists and links are essential elements in HTML for structuring content and providing navigation. Lists help organize information, while hyperlinks allow users to navigate between pages, access external resources, and interact with your website's content. Understanding how to create effective lists and links is crucial for creating user-friendly and organized web content.

3.5 Comments in HTML

Comments in HTML are not visible to users but serve as annotations or notes within the HTML code. They are useful for documenting your code, providing explanations, or temporarily disabling code without removing it. HTML comments are enclosed within <!-- and --> delimiters and can span multiple lines. In this section, we'll explore how to use comments effectively in HTML.

Syntax of HTML Comments

HTML comments follow a specific syntax. Here's how you create an HTML comment:

```
<!-- This is a comment -->
```

- The <!-- sequence marks the beginning of the comment.
- The --> sequence marks the end of the comment.
- Anything between these delimiters is considered a comment and is not rendered in the web page.

Using Comments for Documentation

One common use of HTML comments is to provide documentation or explanations for parts of your code. This can be particularly helpful when working on a team or when revisiting your code after some time. For example:

```
<!-- Header section with logo and navigation -->
<div id="header">
  <img src="logo.png" alt="Company Logo">
  <nav>
    <ul>
```

```
      <li><a href="/">Home</a></li>
      <li><a href="/about">About Us</a></li>
      <li><a href="/contact">Contact</a></li>
    </ul>
  </nav>
</div>
```

In the above example, the comment provides context about the purpose of the `<div>` element with the ID "header."

Commenting Out Code

HTML comments are also useful for temporarily disabling or "commenting out" code without deleting it. This can be handy when you want to test how your web page looks or behaves without a specific section of code. For example:

```
<!-- This image is causing layout issues
<img src="problematic-image.png" alt="Problematic Image">
-->
```

By surrounding the problematic code with comments, it becomes inactive, and you can easily uncomment it later to re-enable it.

Conditional Comments

In older versions of Internet Explorer (prior to IE 11), conditional comments were used to target specific versions of the browser. While they are not part of the HTML standard, they were widely used for browser-specific CSS and JavaScript. Conditional comments typically looked like this:

```
<!--[if IE 9]>
<link rel="stylesheet" type="text/css" href="ie9-styles.css">
<![endif]-->
```

However, conditional comments are no longer supported in modern versions of Internet Explorer and are not recommended for use.

Best Practices for Using HTML Comments

Here are some best practices for using HTML comments effectively:

1. **Be Clear and Concise**: Write comments that provide valuable information without being overly verbose.

2. **Use Comments Sparingly**: While comments are helpful, avoid excessive commenting, as it can clutter your code.

3. **Keep Comments Updated**: If you make changes to the code, remember to update any relevant comments.

4. **Avoid Comments for Obvious Code**: You don't need to comment on code that is self-explanatory.

5. **Use Comments for Problematic Code**: Comment out code that you suspect may be causing issues to troubleshoot later.

6. **Remove Unused Comments**: Periodically review your code and remove unnecessary comments to keep it clean.

In summary, HTML comments are a valuable tool for documenting, explaining, and managing your HTML code. When used judiciously, they can improve code readability and maintainability.

Chapter 4: Text Formatting and Styling

4.1 Formatting Text with HTML

HTML provides a variety of elements and attributes that allow you to format and style text within your web pages. Proper text formatting can enhance the readability and visual appeal of your content. In this section, we'll explore some of the fundamental HTML elements and techniques for text formatting.

1. Bold Text (`<strong>`)

The `<strong>` element is used to indicate that text should be displayed in a bold font weight, typically for emphasizing its importance. It is a semantic HTML element that conveys the significance of the enclosed text:

```
<p>This is a <strong>bold</strong> word.</p>
```

The above code will render as: "This is a **bold** word."

2. Italic Text (`<em>`)

The `<em>` element is used to indicate that text should be displayed in an italicized font style, typically for emphasizing or providing emphasis to specific words or phrases:

```
<p>This is an <em>italic</em> word.</p>
```

The above code will render as: "This is an *italic* word."

3. Underlined Text (`<u>`)

While not a recommended practice for general text styling, the `<u>` element can be used to underline text. However, it is more common to use CSS for text decoration. Nonetheless, here's how you can underline text using HTML:

```
<p>This is an <u>underlined</u> word.</p>
```

The above code will render as: "This is an underlined word."

4. Strikethrough Text (`<s>`)

The `<s>` element is used to indicate text that has been struck through, typically to represent deleted or obsolete content:

```
<p>This is a <s>struck-through</s> word.</p>
```

The above code will render as: "This is a ~~struck-through~~ word."

5. Subscript and Superscript Text (`<sub>` and `<sup>`)

The `<sub>` and `<sup>` elements are used for subscript and superscript text, respectively. Subscript is commonly used for chemical formulas and mathematical equations, while superscript is used for footnotes and exponents:

```html
<p>H<sub>2</sub>O is a chemical formula.</p>
<p>2<sup>3</sup> equals 8.</p>
```

The above code will render as: - "H_2O is a chemical formula." - "2^3 equals 8."

6. Marked Text (`<mark>`)

The `<mark>` element is used to highlight or mark specific portions of text, often used to indicate search results or important keywords:

```html
<p>You can <mark>highlight</mark> important terms in your document.</p>
```

The above code will render with the word "highlight" highlighted.

7. Abbreviations and Acronyms (`<abbr>`)

The `<abbr>` element is used to define and format abbreviations or acronyms, typically by displaying them with a dotted underline and providing a tooltip with the full expansion of the abbreviation:

```html
<p><abbr title="HyperText Markup Language">HTML</abbr> is used for web develo
pment.</p>
```

When users hover over "HTML," they may see a tooltip displaying "HyperText Markup Language."

These are some of the basic HTML elements for text formatting. While HTML can achieve simple text formatting, more advanced styling is often accomplished using CSS (Cascading Style Sheets). CSS provides greater control over fonts, colors, spacing, and other text styles, allowing you to create visually appealing and consistent web designs. In the next sections, we'll explore CSS for styling HTML content in more detail.

4.2 Working with Fonts and Colors

In web design, typography plays a crucial role in conveying your content effectively and creating a visually appealing layout. HTML and CSS provide various tools for working with fonts and colors to style your text. In this section, we'll explore how to set fonts and colors for your web content.

Setting Fonts with CSS

CSS (Cascading Style Sheets) allows you to specify font styles for text elements on your web page. You can define fonts for specific elements or apply styles globally.

Font families define the typefaces that should be used for text. Common font families include "Arial," "Times New Roman," "Helvetica," "Georgia," and more. You can set a font family using the font-family property in CSS:

```
body {
    font-family: Arial, sans-serif;
}
```

In the example above, we set the default font for the entire body element to "Arial." If "Arial" is not available, the browser will use the generic sans-serif font.

Font Size

You can control the size of your text using the font-size property in CSS. Font sizes can be specified in various units, such as pixels (px), ems (em), or percentages (%):

```
h1 {
    font-size: 24px;
}
```

```
p {
    font-size: 16px;
}
```

The above code sets the font size for <h1> elements to 24 pixels and for <p> elements to 16 pixels.

Font Weight

Font weight determines how bold or thin text appears. You can use the font-weight property in CSS to specify different font weights, such as "normal," "bold," or numeric values:

```
strong {
    font-weight: bold;
}
```

```
em {
    font-weight: normal;
}
```

In this example, the <strong> element will be displayed in a bold font weight, while the <em> element will use the normal font weight.

Setting Text Colors with CSS

Colors are another essential aspect of text styling. You can specify text colors using the color property in CSS. Colors can be represented in various formats, including color names, hexadecimal codes, RGB values, and HSL values.

You can use predefined color names in CSS to set text colors. Common color names include "red," "blue," "green," "black," and many more:

```
a {
  color: blue;
}
```

```
p {
  color: darkred;
}
```

In this code, links (`<a>`) will appear in blue text, while paragraphs (`<p>`) will have dark red text.

Using Hexadecimal Codes

Hexadecimal color codes offer a wide range of color choices. They are specified with a hash (#) followed by six hexadecimal digits representing the color's red, green, and blue (RGB) values:

```
h2 {
  color: #FF5733;
}
```

The above code sets the text color of `<h2>` elements to a shade of orange.

Using RGB Values

RGB values allow precise control over the intensity of red, green, and blue components. You can specify text colors using the `rgb()` function:

```
blockquote {
  color: rgb(100, 149, 237);
}
```

In this example, text within `<blockquote>` elements will appear in a shade of blue.

Using HSL Values

HSL (Hue, Saturation, Lightness) values provide a different way to define colors. The `hsl()` function allows you to set text colors based on hue, saturation, and lightness:

```
code {
  color: hsl(120, 100%, 50%);
}
```

Here, the text color of `<code>` elements will be a bright green.

You can combine font styles and colors to achieve various text effects. For example:

```
blockquote {
  font-style: italic;
  color: #333;
}
```

In this code, text within `<blockquote>` elements will be italicized and have a dark gray color.

In summary, working with fonts and colors is an essential part of web typography. CSS provides the flexibility to control the appearance of text elements, allowing you to create visually appealing and well-styled web content. Proper font and color choices can greatly enhance the readability and aesthetics of your web pages.

4.3 CSS for Styling HTML

Cascading Style Sheets (CSS) are a powerful tool for styling HTML elements and controlling the layout and presentation of your web content. In this section, we'll explore how CSS works and how you can use it to style HTML elements.

Understanding CSS Syntax

CSS uses a simple syntax that consists of two main parts: selectors and declarations.

- **Selectors**: Selectors target HTML elements to which you want to apply styles. They can target specific elements, classes, IDs, or even pseudo-classes like `:hover`.

- **Declarations**: Declarations define the styles you want to apply to the selected elements. Each declaration consists of a property and a value separated by a colon (`:`), and declarations are enclosed in curly braces `{}`.

Here's a basic CSS rule with a selector and a declaration:

```
selector {
  property: value;
}
```

For example, to change the color of all `<p>` elements to blue, you can use the following CSS rule:

```
p {
  color: blue;
}
```

CSS Selectors

CSS provides various types of selectors to target HTML elements. Here are some common selectors:

- **Element Selector**: Targets all instances of a specific HTML element. For example, p targets all paragraphs.

- **Class Selector**: Targets elements with a specific class attribute. For example, .highlight targets all elements with the class="highlight" attribute.

- **ID Selector**: Targets a specific element with a unique ID attribute. For example, #header targets the element with id="header".

- **Descendant Selector**: Targets an element that is a descendant of another element. For example, ul li targets all <li> elements that are descendants of <ul> elements.

- **Pseudo-class Selector**: Targets elements in specific states or conditions. For example, a:hover targets links when they are hovered over.

Applying CSS Styles

CSS styles can be applied to HTML elements in several ways:

1. **Inline Styles**: You can apply styles directly to individual HTML elements using the style attribute. For example:

```
<p style="color: red; font-size: 16px;">This is a red, 16px text.</p>
```

2. **Internal CSS**: You can include CSS within a <style> block in the <head> section of your HTML document. This style block contains CSS rules that apply to the entire document:

```
<head>
  <style>
    p {
      color: green;
      font-size: 18px;
    }
  </style>
</head>
```

3. **External CSS**: You can create a separate CSS file (usually with a .css extension) and link it to your HTML document using the <link> element. This is the most common way to apply styles to a website. Here's an example:

```
<head>
  <link rel="stylesheet" type="text/css" href="styles.css">
</head>
```

CSS offers a wide range of properties for controlling the appearance of elements. Some common CSS properties include:

- color: Sets the text color.
- background-color: Sets the background color.
- font-family: Defines the font type.
- font-size: Specifies the font size.
- font-weight: Controls the font weight (e.g., bold).
- text-align: Aligns text (left, right, center).
- margin and padding: Set spacing around elements.
- border: Adds borders to elements.
- width and height: Defines element dimensions.
- display: Specifies how an element is displayed (e.g., block or inline).

CSS Box Model

The CSS box model is a fundamental concept in web design. It defines how elements are rendered in terms of content, padding, border, and margin. Understanding the box model is crucial for controlling the spacing and layout of elements on a webpage.

CSS Specificity

CSS specificity determines which styles are applied when multiple conflicting styles target the same element. Specificity is based on the combination of selectors and their order in the CSS file.

In summary, CSS is a powerful tool for styling HTML content. It allows you to control the appearance, layout, and presentation of elements on your web pages. Understanding CSS syntax, selectors, properties, and the box model is essential for creating visually appealing and well-structured web designs.

4.4 Text Alignment and Spacing

Text alignment and spacing are essential aspects of web typography and layout. They determine how text is positioned within its containing element and how space is distributed around it. In this section, we'll explore text alignment and spacing techniques using CSS.

Text Alignment

Text alignment defines how text is horizontally positioned within its container. CSS provides several properties to control text alignment:

- **text-align**: This property sets the horizontal alignment of text within its container. Common values include "left," "right," "center," and "justify."

```
p {
  text-align: center;
}
```

The above CSS rule centers the text within all <p> elements.

Line Height

Line height, also known as leading, controls the vertical space between lines of text. It's an important factor in readability and aesthetics. You can set line height using the line-height property:

```
p {
  line-height: 1.5;
}
```

In this example, the line height of text within <p> elements is set to 1.5 times the font size.

Letter Spacing

Letter spacing, or kerning, defines the space between individual characters in text. You can control letter spacing using the letter-spacing property:

```
h1 {
  letter-spacing: 2px;
}
```

The above CSS rule increases the space between characters in <h1> elements by 2 pixels.

Word Spacing

Word spacing determines the space between words in a block of text. You can set word spacing using the word-spacing property:

```
blockquote {
  word-spacing: 4px;
}
```

This CSS rule increases the space between words in <blockquote> elements by 4 pixels.

Text Indentation

Text indentation controls the space before the first line of text in an element. You can set text indentation using the text-indent property:

```
ul {
  text-indent: 20px;
}
```

In this example, the text within <ul> elements is indented by 20 pixels from the left.

Text Alignment in Tables

Text alignment can also be applied to table cells and their content. CSS properties like `text-align` and `vertical-align` are used to control the alignment of text and content within table cells.

For example, to center text horizontally and vertically within a table cell:

```
td {
  text-align: center;
  vertical-align: middle;
}
```

The above CSS rule ensures that text within table cells (`<td>`) is centered both horizontally and vertically.

Text Shadow

Text shadow is a CSS property that allows you to add a shadow effect to text. It can enhance the visibility and style of text on your web page. The `text-shadow` property accepts values for horizontal and vertical offsets, blur radius, and shadow color.

```
h2 {
  text-shadow: 2px 2px 4px rgba(0, 0, 0, 0.5);
}
```

In this example, `<h2>` elements will have a text shadow that is 2 pixels to the right, 2 pixels down, with a blur radius of 4 pixels, and a shadow color with 50% opacity.

Text Alignment and Accessibility

When using text alignment and spacing properties, it's essential to consider accessibility. Proper alignment and spacing can improve readability for all users, including those with visual impairments. Avoid excessive text indentation or letter spacing that may hinder readability. Additionally, use semantic HTML elements and maintain a logical reading order in your content.

In summary, text alignment and spacing properties in CSS allow you to control how text is positioned and formatted within your web page. Proper use of these properties can enhance the visual appeal and readability of your content, but it's essential to consider accessibility guidelines when applying text styles and layouts.

4.5 Using External Stylesheets

Using external stylesheets is a common and efficient way to manage the styling of your HTML documents. Instead of embedding CSS directly into your HTML files, you can create a separate CSS file and link it to your HTML documents. In this section, we'll explore the benefits and steps of using external stylesheets.

Benefits of External Stylesheets

1. **Separation of Concerns**: External stylesheets promote the separation of content (HTML), presentation (CSS), and behavior (JavaScript). This separation makes your code more organized and maintainable.

2. **Reusability**: You can reuse the same stylesheet across multiple HTML pages, ensuring consistent styling throughout your website.

3. **Ease of Maintenance**: Modifying styles is more straightforward when they are centralized in one CSS file. You can make changes globally without editing each HTML file individually.

4. **Caching**: Browsers can cache external stylesheets, resulting in faster page load times for returning visitors.

5. **Reduced File Size**: External stylesheets can be cached and shared across multiple pages, reducing the overall file size of your website. This can lead to faster loading times for users.

Creating an External Stylesheet

To create an external stylesheet, follow these steps:

1. **Create a New CSS File**: Use a text editor to create a new file with a `.css` extension. For example, you can name it `styles.css`.

2. **Write Your CSS**: In the `.css` file, write your CSS rules as you would in an internal stylesheet. For example:

```css
/* styles.css */

body {
    font-family: Arial, sans-serif;
    background-color: #f0f0f0;
}

h1 {
    color: #333;
}
```

3. **Save the CSS File**: Save the file in the same directory as your HTML files or in a designated folder for stylesheets.

Linking the External Stylesheet to HTML

To link the external stylesheet to your HTML documents, use the `<link>` element in the `<head>` section of your HTML file. Here's the code to link the `styles.css` stylesheet:

```html
<!DOCTYPE html>
<html>
```

```
<head>
  <link rel="stylesheet" type="text/css" href="styles.css">
</head>
<body>
  <!-- Your HTML content goes here -->
</body>
</html>
```

In the `<link>` element: - `rel="stylesheet"` specifies that the linked file is a stylesheet. - `type="text/css"` specifies the type of content in the linked file (CSS). - `href="styles.css"` specifies the path to the external CSS file.

Using the External Stylesheet

Once linked, the external stylesheet will apply its styles to the HTML elements in the same way as an internal stylesheet. You can use HTML elements, classes, IDs, or other selectors to apply styles defined in the external CSS file.

Benefits of External Stylesheets for Large Projects

For larger web projects with multiple HTML files and complex styling requirements, external stylesheets are especially advantageous. They promote maintainability, consistency, and efficient collaboration among developers and designers. By centralizing your styles in one place, you can easily update, modify, and expand your website's design without the need to sift through numerous HTML files.

In summary, using external stylesheets is a best practice in web development. It offers several benefits, including code organization, reusability, ease of maintenance, and improved performance. By linking an external stylesheet to your HTML documents, you can efficiently manage the presentation of your web content.

Chapter 5: Working with Images and Multimedia

5.1 Adding Images to Your Web Page

Images are a crucial component of web design, as they enhance visual appeal and engage users. In this section, we'll explore how to add images to your web pages using HTML.

The `<img>` Element

To display images on a web page, you can use the `<img>` (image) element in HTML. The `<img>` element is an empty, self-closing tag that requires a few attributes to specify the image source and alternative text.

Image Source (src)

The `src` attribute specifies the source (URL) of the image file. It can be a local file path or a web URL. Here's an example of how to use the `src` attribute:

```
<img src="image.jpg" alt="A beautiful landscape">
```

In this example, the image file "image.jpg" is displayed on the web page. The `alt` attribute provides alternative text that is shown if the image cannot be loaded or for accessibility purposes.

Alternative Text (alt)

The `alt` attribute (short for "alternative text") is used to describe the image's content for users who cannot see the image, such as screen reader users or when the image fails to load. Providing meaningful alternative text is essential for web accessibility and SEO (Search Engine Optimization). Here's how to use the `alt` attribute:

```
<img src="flower.jpg" alt="A close-up of a beautiful red rose">
```

In this example, the `alt` attribute describes the image as a "close-up of a beautiful red rose."

Image Dimensions (width and height)

You can use the `width` and `height` attributes to specify the dimensions (in pixels) of the displayed image. These attributes are optional, but setting them can help control the layout of your web page and improve page loading performance. Here's how to use the `width` and `height` attributes:

```
<img src="logo.png" alt="Company Logo" width="200" height="100">
```

In this code, the image is set to have a width of 200 pixels and a height of 100 pixels.

When specifying the `src` attribute, you can use either a relative or an absolute path to the image file:

- **Relative Path**: A relative path points to the image file relative to the location of the HTML file. For example, if the HTML file and the image are in the same directory, you can use a relative path like `src="image.jpg"`.

- **Absolute Path**: An absolute path specifies the full URL or file path to the image, regardless of the HTML file's location. For example, `src="https://example.com/images/image.jpg"` is an absolute path to an image hosted on a remote server.

Image Formats

Web images come in various formats, each with its own characteristics and best use cases. Common image formats include:

- **JPEG (or JPG)**: Suitable for photographs and images with many colors. It offers good compression but may lose some quality.

- **PNG**: Ideal for images with transparency or sharp edges, such as logos and icons. It supports lossless compression.

- **GIF**: Often used for animated images. It has limited colors and is best for simple animations.

- **SVG**: Scalable Vector Graphics are ideal for logos and icons that need to be scalable without loss of quality.

Image Accessibility

When adding images to your web page, it's essential to consider accessibility. Provide descriptive and meaningful alternative text using the `alt` attribute to ensure that users with disabilities can understand the image's content. Additionally, use proper image dimensions and file formats to optimize accessibility and performance.

In summary, the `<img>` element allows you to include images in your web pages. Specify the image source with the `src` attribute, provide alternative text with the `alt` attribute, and consider using the `width` and `height` attributes for layout control. Ensure that your images are accessible to all users by providing descriptive alternative text.

5.2 Image Attributes and Optimization

When working with images on the web, it's important to understand image attributes and how to optimize your images for better performance and user experience. In this section, we'll explore various image attributes and techniques for image optimization.

The src Attribute

As mentioned in the previous section, the `src` attribute in the `<img>` element specifies the source (URL) of the image file. It's essential to provide the correct path to the image you want to display. Incorrect or broken paths can result in missing images on your web page.

```
<img src="image.jpg" alt="A beautiful landscape">
```

The alt Attribute

The `alt` attribute is used to provide alternative text for images. It is crucial for web accessibility, as it allows screen readers to describe the image to users who cannot see it. When adding alternative text, be descriptive and concise to convey the image's content or purpose.

```
<img src="flower.jpg" alt="A close-up of a beautiful red rose">
```

The width and height Attributes

The `width` and `height` attributes in the `<img>` element specify the dimensions (in pixels) of the displayed image. Setting these attributes is optional but can be beneficial for controlling the layout of your web page and optimizing page loading performance.

```
<img src="logo.png" alt="Company Logo" width="200" height="100">
```

Specifying the image dimensions helps the browser allocate space for the image before it loads, preventing content from jumping around as images load.

Image File Formats

Choosing the right image file format is crucial for web performance and quality. Common image formats include:

- **JPEG (or JPG)**: Suitable for photographs and images with many colors. It offers good compression but may lose some quality.

- **PNG**: Ideal for images with transparency or sharp edges, such as logos and icons. It supports lossless compression.

- **GIF**: Often used for animated images. It has limited colors and is best for simple animations.

- **SVG**: Scalable Vector Graphics are ideal for logos and icons that need to be scalable without loss of quality.

Select the image format that best suits your content and consider compression techniques to reduce file size without compromising quality.

Image Compression

Image compression reduces the file size of images, making them load faster on web pages. There are two main types of image compression:

- **Lossless Compression**: This method reduces file size without sacrificing image quality. It's suitable for images that require high detail and clarity.

- **Lossy Compression**: Lossy compression sacrifices some image quality to achieve significant file size reduction. It's commonly used for photographs and images where slight quality loss is acceptable.

To compress images, you can use various tools and software, or you can opt for online image compression services.

Responsive Images

Responsive web design aims to provide an optimal viewing experience across different devices and screen sizes. To achieve this, you can use responsive images. One way to create responsive images is by specifying multiple image sources using the srcset attribute in the <img> element. The browser then selects the most appropriate image source based on the user's device and screen characteristics.

```
<img
  srcset="image-small.jpg 320w, image-medium.jpg 640w, image-large.jpg 1200w"
  sizes="(max-width: 480px) 100vw, (max-width: 768px) 50vw, 33vw"
  src="image-medium.jpg"
  alt="Responsive Image"
>
```

In this example, different image sources are provided with their widths, and the sizes attribute defines how the image should be displayed on various screen sizes.

Lazy Loading

Lazy loading is a technique that defers the loading of images until they are near the user's viewport. This can significantly improve page loading times, especially for pages with multiple large images. To implement lazy loading, you can use the loading="lazy" attribute in the <img> element.

```
<img src="image.jpg" alt="Lazy Loaded Image" loading="lazy">
```

Image Accessibility and SEO

When optimizing images, don't forget to consider accessibility and SEO. Ensure that you provide meaningful alternative text using the alt attribute for all images. Descriptive alternative text helps users with disabilities understand the content of images and improves SEO by providing context to search engines.

In summary, understanding image attributes and optimizing your images for the web is essential for delivering a fast and accessible user experience. Proper use of attributes like `alt`, `width`, and `height`, along with image compression techniques, can significantly improve web page performance. Additionally, responsive images and lazy loading are valuable techniques for modern web design.

5.3 Embedding Audio and Video

In addition to images, modern web pages often include audio and video elements to provide multimedia content and enhance user engagement. HTML5 introduced native support for embedding audio and video directly into web pages using the `<audio>` and `<video>` elements. In this section, we'll explore how to embed audio and video content in your web pages.

The `<audio>` Element

The `<audio>` element allows you to embed audio files, such as music or podcasts, directly into your web page. To use the `<audio>` element, you specify the source of the audio file using the `src` attribute.

```
<audio src="audio.mp3" controls>
   Your browser does not support the audio element.
</audio>
```

In this example, an audio file named "audio.mp3" is embedded into the web page. The `controls` attribute adds audio playback controls, allowing users to play, pause, adjust the volume, and more.

Supported Audio Formats

Different web browsers support various audio formats. To ensure compatibility, consider providing multiple source formats using the `<source>` element within the `<audio>` element. Browsers will choose the supported format automatically.

```
<audio controls>
   <source src="audio.mp3" type="audio/mpeg">
   <source src="audio.ogg" type="audio/ogg">
   Your browser does not support the audio element.
</audio>
```

In this code, both MP3 and OGG audio formats are provided. The browser will select the format it can play.

The `<video>` Element

The `<video>` element is used for embedding video content, such as movies, tutorials, or webinars, directly into your web page. Similar to the `<audio>` element, you specify the source of the video file using the `src` attribute.

```
<video src="video.mp4" controls>
  Your browser does not support the video element.
</video>
```

In this example, a video file named "video.mp4" is embedded, and the `controls` attribute adds video playback controls.

Just like with audio, various web browsers support different video formats. To ensure broad compatibility, provide multiple source formats using the `<source>` element within the `<video>` element.

```
<video controls>
  <source src="video.mp4" type="video/mp4">
  <source src="video.webm" type="video/webm">
  Your browser does not support the video element.
</video>
```

In this code, both MP4 and WebM video formats are provided. The browser will select the format it can play.

Additional Attributes

Both `<audio>` and `<video>` elements support several attributes that allow you to customize the media playback experience:

- **autoplay**: This attribute automatically starts media playback as soon as the media element is loaded.

- **loop**: When set, the media will loop continuously, replaying once it reaches the end.

- **preload**: This attribute controls how much of the media file is loaded before playback begins. Values can be "auto," "metadata," or "none."

- **poster**: The `poster` attribute specifies an image to be displayed while the media is downloading or until the user starts playing it. It's especially useful for videos.

Responsive Media

To make audio and video elements responsive to different screen sizes, you can use CSS to style and size them accordingly. Consider using CSS media queries to adjust the dimensions of media elements for different screen widths or orientations.

Accessibility

When embedding audio and video content, it's crucial to consider accessibility. Provide descriptive text or transcripts for audio and video content to make it accessible to users with disabilities. Additionally, ensure that your media controls and playback functionality are keyboard accessible.

In summary, HTML5 provides native support for embedding audio and video content in web pages using the <audio> and <video> elements. You can customize the playback experience with attributes like autoplay and loop, and ensure compatibility by providing multiple source formats. Consider accessibility when adding multimedia content to your web pages to make it inclusive for all users.

5.4 HTML5 Multimedia Elements

HTML5 introduced several multimedia elements that enhance the way audio and video content is integrated into web pages. These elements provide better support for media playback, streaming, and interaction. In this section, we'll explore some of these HTML5 multimedia elements.

The <audio> Element

The <audio> element, introduced earlier, allows you to embed audio files into web pages. HTML5 introduced additional features and capabilities for this element, such as the ability to play audio without visible controls and control audio playback programmatically using JavaScript.

Audio Without Controls

You can create an audio player without visible controls by omitting the controls attribute. In this case, you'll need to use JavaScript to control audio playback, making it suitable for custom audio experiences.

```
<audio id="customAudio">
  <source src="audio.mp3" type="audio/mpeg">
  Your browser does not support the audio element.
</audio>

<button onclick="playAudio()">Play</button>
<button onclick="pauseAudio()">Pause</button>

<script>
  const audio = document.getElementById("customAudio");

  function playAudio() {
    audio.play();
  }

  function pauseAudio() {
    audio.pause();
  }
</script>
```

In this example, the audio element has no visible controls. Instead, JavaScript functions are used to control audio playback with "Play" and "Pause" buttons.

The <video> Element

Similarly, the <video> element has evolved in HTML5 to support various features and customization options beyond basic video playback.

Video Captions and Subtitles

HTML5 introduced the <track> element, which allows you to provide captions and subtitles for videos. You can specify the language and kind of text track, whether it's captions, subtitles, or descriptions.

```
<video controls>
    <source src="video.mp4" type="video/mp4">
    <track src="captions.vtt" kind="subtitles" srclang="en" label="English">
    Your browser does not support the video element.
</video>
```

In this code, a subtitles track in the WebVTT format is provided, enhancing the accessibility of the video.

Video Preload Options

The preload attribute in the <video> element allows you to control how much of the video is loaded before playback begins. You can set it to "auto," "metadata," or "none." For example:

```
<video preload="auto" controls>
    <source src="video.mp4" type="video/mp4">
    Your browser does not support the video element.
</video>
```

Setting preload="auto" instructs the browser to start loading the video as soon as possible.

The <source> Element

The <source> element is used within the <audio> and <video> elements to specify multiple sources for media files. This ensures cross-browser compatibility and allows the browser to choose the most suitable source based on its capabilities.

```
<video controls>
    <source src="video.mp4" type="video/mp4">
    <source src="video.webm" type="video/webm">
    Your browser does not support the video element.
</video>
```

In this example, both MP4 and WebM video formats are provided, and the browser will select the format it can play.

The <canvas> Element

While not a multimedia playback element, the <canvas> element introduced in HTML5 is essential for creating dynamic graphics and animations, which can enhance multimedia experiences. You can use JavaScript to draw graphics, animations, and interactive elements within a <canvas> element.

```
<canvas id="myCanvas" width="400" height="200"></canvas>

<script>
  const canvas = document.getElementById("myCanvas");
  const context = canvas.getContext("2d");

  // Draw a red rectangle
  context.fillStyle = "red";
  context.fillRect(50, 50, 200, 100);
</script>
```

In this example, a red rectangle is drawn on the canvas using JavaScript. The <canvas> element opens up possibilities for creating interactive multimedia elements on your web page.

In summary, HTML5 introduced several multimedia elements and features that enhance the integration of audio and video content into web pages. The <audio> and <video> elements support various options for customization, accessibility, and cross-browser compatibility. Additionally, the <track> element allows for the inclusion of captions and subtitles, and the <canvas> element enables the creation of dynamic graphics and animations within web pages.

5.5 Responsive Images and Media

In today's multi-device world, creating web content that adapts to various screen sizes and resolutions is crucial. Responsive web design ensures that your images and media scale and adjust appropriately, providing the best user experience on different devices. In this section, we'll explore responsive techniques for images and media.

The Need for Responsive Design

Responsive design is a design approach that aims to make web content look and function well on a variety of devices, including desktop computers, laptops, tablets, and smartphones. To achieve this, responsive design involves adjusting layouts, fonts, images, and media to fit the device's screen size and orientation.

Responsive Images

Images often need to be scaled and optimized for different screen sizes and resolutions. HTML provides several techniques for creating responsive images:

1. The srcset Attribute

The `srcset` attribute allows you to specify multiple image sources with different resolutions or sizes. Browsers can then choose the most appropriate source based on the user's device capabilities. You can also use the `sizes` attribute to provide additional information about how the image should be displayed.

```html
<img
    srcset="image-small.jpg 320w, image-medium.jpg 640w, image-large.jpg 1200w"
    sizes="(max-width: 480px) 100vw, (max-width: 768px) 50vw, 33vw"
    src="image-medium.jpg"
    alt="Responsive Image"
>
```

In this example, different image sources are specified along with their widths, and the `sizes` attribute defines how the image should be displayed on various screen sizes.

2. CSS for Responsive Images

CSS can be used to make images responsive by setting their maximum width to 100%. This ensures that images scale down to fit their parent container while maintaining their aspect ratio.

```css
img {
    max-width: 100%;
    height: auto;
}
```

By using this CSS rule, you ensure that images won't exceed the width of their container, preventing horizontal scrollbars on smaller screens.

Responsive Video

Responsive design principles can also be applied to video elements. Ensuring that videos adapt to different screen sizes and orientations is essential for providing a seamless user experience.

Video Width and Height

To make videos responsive, you can set the `width` to 100% and `height` to auto. This allows videos to scale proportionally within their parent containers.

```html
<video width="100%" height="auto" controls>
    <source src="video.mp4" type="video/mp4">
    Your browser does not support the video element.
</video>
```

By setting the width to 100%, the video element will adapt to the available width while maintaining its aspect ratio.

CSS Flexbox and Grid layout systems are powerful tools for creating responsive designs for both images and media. You can use these layout systems to control the positioning and arrangement of images and media elements within your web page's layout.

```css
.container {
  display: flex;
  flex-wrap: wrap;
  justify-content: space-between;
}

.image {
  flex: 1;
  margin: 10px;
}
```

In this example, a container is created with Flexbox, and individual images within the container can adapt to different screen sizes and orientations.

Media Queries

Media queries are CSS rules that allow you to apply styles based on the characteristics of the user's device, such as screen width or orientation. They are a fundamental part of responsive design.

```css
@media screen and (max-width: 768px) {
  /* CSS rules for screens with a maximum width of 768px */
}

@media screen and (orientation: landscape) {
  /* CSS rules for landscape orientation */
}
```

Media queries can be used to change the layout, font sizes, and other styles to optimize the user experience on various devices.

Testing and Debugging

To ensure the responsiveness of your web content, it's essential to test your designs on different devices and screen sizes. Many modern web browsers come with built-in developer tools that allow you to simulate various devices and screen resolutions for testing.

In summary, creating responsive images and media is a critical aspect of modern web design. By using techniques like the srcset attribute, CSS rules, and media queries, you can ensure that your web content looks and functions well on a wide range of devices, providing an optimal user experience. Testing and debugging on different devices are essential steps in ensuring the effectiveness of your responsive design.

Chapter 6: Hyperlinks and Navigation

6.1 Creating Hyperlinks

Hyperlinks, often referred to as links, are an essential part of web development. They allow you to connect web pages and enable users to navigate the web by clicking on them. In this section, we'll explore how to create hyperlinks in HTML and understand the different types of links you can use.

The Anchor Element

In HTML, hyperlinks are created using the anchor element `<a>`. The anchor element defines a clickable link that can take users to another web page, a different section of the same page, or even external resources like documents and email addresses.

Here's the basic structure of an anchor element:

```
<a href="URL">Link Text</a>
```

- **href**: The `href` attribute specifies the URL (Uniform Resource Locator) where the link points to. It can be an absolute URL (e.g., `https://www.example.com`) or a relative URL (e.g., `page.html` or `../other-page.html`).

- **Link Text**: The text enclosed within the `<a>` tags is the visible part of the link that users can click on. This text is known as the anchor text.

Let's look at some examples of how to create different types of hyperlinks:

1. Creating a Basic Link

```
<a href="https://www.example.com">Visit Example.com</a>
```

In this example, clicking on the "Visit Example.com" link will take the user to the `https://www.example.com` website.

2. Creating a Relative Link

```
<a href="page.html">Go to Page</a>
```

This creates a link to a page within the same website. The browser will navigate to the `page.html` file within the current website's directory.

3. Linking to an Email Address

You can use the `mailto` scheme to create links that open the user's default email client with a pre-filled email address. For example:

```
<a href="mailto:contact@example.com">Email Us</a>
```

Clicking on the "Email Us" link will open the user's email client with the recipient's address set to `contact@example.com`.

Linking to Sections within a Page

Hyperlinks can also be used to link to different sections within the same web page. To do this, you'll need to use anchor tags with id attributes to mark the target sections, and then create links to those sections using the href attribute.

Creating an Anchor Point
```
<a id="section1"></a>
```

In this example, we've created an anchor point with the id attribute set to "section1."

Creating a Link to the Anchor Point
```
<a href="#section1">Jump to Section 1</a>
```

This link will take the user to the section with the "section1" anchor point when clicked.

Targeting Links

By default, when a user clicks on a link, the linked content replaces the current content in the same browser window or tab. However, you can control the behavior of links using the target attribute.

Opening Links in a New Tab/Window
```
<a href="https://www.example.com" target="_blank">Open in New Tab</a>
```

The target="_blank" attribute-value pair tells the browser to open the linked content in a new browser tab or window.

Styling Links with CSS

You can apply CSS styles to hyperlinks to make them visually distinct and fit the design of your website. Common styles include changing the color, underlining, and adding hover effects to links.

```
a {
    color: #0078d4; /* Change link color */
    text-decoration: none; /* Remove underline */
}

a:hover {
    text-decoration: underline; /* Add underline on hover */
}
```

These CSS rules change the link color to blue and remove the underline by default. On hover, the underline is added back to the link text.

Summary

Creating hyperlinks in HTML is essential for connecting web pages and providing navigation options for users. The anchor element <a> is used to define links, and the href attribute specifies the URL or target location. You can create links to external websites, other pages within your site, or even sections within the same page. Additionally, you can control link behavior using the `target` attribute and style links with CSS to match your website's design.

In the next sections, we'll explore more advanced topics related to hyperlinks and navigation, including relative and absolute URLs, navigation menus, and styling links with CSS.

6.2 Relative vs. Absolute URLs

When creating hyperlinks in HTML, you have the option to use either relative or absolute URLs to specify the destination of the link. Understanding the difference between these two types of URLs is crucial for effective web development and navigation.

Absolute URLs

An absolute URL provides the complete address of the linked resource, including the protocol (e.g., `http` or `https`), domain name (e.g., `www.example.com`), and the path to the specific resource (e.g., `/page.html`). Here's an example of an absolute URL:

```
<a href="https://www.example.com/page.html">Visit Example Page</a>
```

Absolute URLs are beneficial when linking to external websites, resources on different domains, or specific pages on your own domain. They provide an explicit and unambiguous reference to the resource's location.

Relative URLs

Relative URLs, on the other hand, specify the path to the linked resource relative to the current page's location. They are typically used when linking to pages within the same website or directory structure. Relative URLs are shorter and more concise than absolute URLs because they don't include the full domain and protocol.

Relative URL Structure

A relative URL can take several forms:

- Relative to the current directory: `"page.html"`
- One directory up: `"../other-page.html"`
- In a subdirectory: `"subdirectory/page.html"`

Here are some examples of relative URLs in anchor elements:

```
<a href="page.html">Go to Page</a>
<a href="../other-page.html">Go to Another Page</a>
<a href="subdirectory/page.html">Go to Subdirectory Page</a>
```

Relative URLs are flexible and make it easier to manage links when moving or restructuring a website. They adapt to the site's structure without needing updates to the full URL.

The choice between absolute and relative URLs depends on the context and purpose of the link:

- **Absolute URLs:** Use absolute URLs when linking to external websites or resources on different domains. They provide an explicit reference and ensure that the link works correctly regardless of the user's location.

- **Relative URLs:** Use relative URLs when linking to pages within your website or subdirectories. They are more concise and adaptable to changes in the site's structure.

Base URL

HTML documents can also include a `<base>` element in the `<head>` section to specify a base URL for all relative URLs within the document. This allows you to set a common reference point for relative links. Here's an example:

```
<head>
  <base href="https://www.example.com/">
</head>
<body>
  <a href="page.html">Go to Page</a> <!-- This link is relative to the base U
RL -->
</body>
```

In this example, the `<base>` element sets the base URL to "`https://www.example.com/`", so the relative link "`page.html`" is interpreted as "`https://www.example.com/page.html`".

Summary

In HTML, you can use either absolute or relative URLs to create hyperlinks. Absolute URLs provide the full address of the linked resource and are suitable for external websites and resources on different domains. Relative URLs specify the path to the linked resource relative to the current page's location and are often used for pages within the same website or directory structure. The choice between them depends on the specific use case and whether you want a fixed or flexible reference to the resource. Additionally, the `<base>` element can be used to set a common base URL for all relative links within an HTML document.

6.3 Linking to Other Pages

Creating hyperlinks to other pages is a fundamental aspect of web development. It allows users to navigate through a website and access various content. In this section, we'll delve deeper into linking to other pages and explore some techniques and best practices.

Relative URLs for Internal Links

When linking to pages within the same website or domain, it's common to use relative URLs. Relative URLs make it easier to maintain links when the website structure changes. Here's an example of linking to another page using a relative URL:

```
<a href="about.html">About Us</a>
```

In this example, the link points to a page named "about.html" located in the same directory as the current page. If you wanted to link to a page in a subdirectory, you would use a relative URL like this:

```
<a href="products/catalog.html">View Our Products</a>
```

This relative URL navigates to a page named "catalog.html" within a subdirectory named "products."

Absolute URLs for External Links

When linking to external websites or resources on different domains, it's essential to use absolute URLs. Absolute URLs include the complete web address, including the protocol (e.g., `https://`), domain name (e.g., `www.example.com`), and the path to the resource. Here's an example:

```
<a href="https://www.example.com">Visit Example Website</a>
```

Absolute URLs ensure that the link functions correctly, regardless of the user's location or the context in which the link is used.

Linking to Email Addresses

HTML allows you to create links that open the user's default email client with a pre-filled email address. To achieve this, you can use the `mailto` scheme in the `href` attribute. Here's an example:

```
<a href="mailto:contact@example.com">Contact Us</a>
```

When the user clicks on this link, it will open their email client with "contact@example.com" as the recipient's email address.

Opening Links in a New Window or Tab

You can control how links open using the `target` attribute. By default, links open in the same window or tab. However, you can use the `target` attribute to specify that a link should open in a new window or tab. Here's an example:

```
<a href="https://www.example.com" target="_blank">Open in New Tab</a>
```

The `target="_blank"` attribute-value pair instructs the browser to open the linked page in a new tab or window.

Linking to Specific Sections on a Page

To create links that navigate to specific sections within a single page, you can use anchor tags with `id` attributes. First, define an `id` for the target section:

```
<div id="section-about">
  <!-- Content of the "About" section -->
</div>
```

Then, create a link to that section using a relative URL with a hash symbol (#):

```
<a href="#section-about">Jump to About</a>
```

When clicked, this link will scroll the page to the section with the "section-about" `id`.

Linking to Files

HTML allows you to link to various file types, such as PDFs, documents, images, and more. To link to a file, specify the file's path in the `href` attribute. For example:

```
<a href="documents/document.pdf">Download PDF</a>
```

This link will allow users to download the "document.pdf" file when clicked.

Best Practices for Linking

Here are some best practices for creating effective and user-friendly links:

- Use clear and descriptive anchor text: Make sure the link text accurately describes the linked content. Avoid generic terms like "click here."

- Test links: Ensure that all links on your website work correctly by regularly testing them.

- Provide visual cues: Use CSS to style links so that they are visually distinguishable from regular text. Common styling includes changing the color, underlining, or adding hover effects.

- Use meaningful URLs: Create meaningful and SEO-friendly URLs that reflect the content of the linked page.

- Consider accessibility: Ensure that links are accessible to users with disabilities by providing appropriate text alternatives.

- Maintain consistency: Keep link styles consistent throughout your website to provide a cohesive user experience.

Summary

Linking to other pages, both within and outside your website, is a crucial part of web development. Understanding the differences between relative and absolute URLs and using them appropriately is essential. Additionally, you can create links to email addresses, open links in new windows or tabs, and link to specific sections within a page. Following best practices for creating effective and user-friendly links will enhance the overall usability and accessibility of your website.

6.4 Navigation Menus and Lists

Navigation menus play a critical role in helping users explore a website and find the content they are looking for. In this section, we'll discuss how to create navigation menus and lists in HTML, providing users with an organized and user-friendly way to navigate your site.

Creating Navigation Menus with Lists

One common way to create navigation menus is by using HTML lists. Lists are versatile and provide a structured way to present links to various sections or pages of your website. There are two main types of HTML lists: unordered lists (<ul>) and ordered lists (<ol>).

Unordered Lists (<ul>)

Unordered lists are typically used for navigation menus where the order of items doesn't matter. Each menu item is represented as a list item (<li>) within the <ul> element. Here's an example:

```
<ul>
  <li><a href="index.html">Home</a></li>
  <li><a href="about.html">About Us</a></li>
  <li><a href="services.html">Services</a></li>
  <li><a href="contact.html">Contact</a></li>
</ul>
```

In this example, we have created an unordered list with four list items, each containing a link to a different page.

Ordered lists are used when the order of items is significant. While they are less common for navigation menus, they can still be employed in cases where a specific order is needed. Here's an example:

```
<ol>
  <li><a href="step1.html">Step 1</a></li>
  <li><a href="step2.html">Step 2</a></li>
  <li><a href="step3.html">Step 3</a></li>
</ol>
```

Styling Navigation Menus with CSS

To make navigation menus visually appealing and user-friendly, you can apply CSS styles to lists and list items. CSS allows you to control aspects like font size, color, spacing, and even the use of background images for menu items.

Here's a basic CSS example that styles an unordered list as a horizontal navigation menu:

```
ul {
  list-style: none; /* Remove bullet points */
  padding: 0; /* Remove default padding */
  display: flex; /* Arrange items in a row */
}

li {
  margin-right: 20px; /* Add spacing between menu items */
}

a {
  text-decoration: none; /* Remove underlines from links */
  color: #333; /* Set link color */
  font-weight: bold; /* Make links bold */
}

a:hover {
  color: #0078d4; /* Change link color on hover */
}
```

This CSS code removes bullet points from the list, arranges list items in a horizontal row, adds spacing between menu items, and styles the links.

Dropdown Menus

In more complex websites, you may need dropdown menus to organize and present a hierarchical structure of pages or sections. Dropdown menus can be implemented using HTML and CSS, often involving nested lists.

Here's a simplified example of an HTML structure for a dropdown menu:

```
<ul>
  <li><a href="index.html">Home</a></li>
  <li>
    <a href="services.html">Services</a>
    <ul>
      <li><a href="web-design.html">Web Design</a></li>
      <li><a href="seo.html">SEO</a></li>
    </ul>
  </li>
  <li><a href="contact.html">Contact</a></li>
</ul>
```

In this example, the "Services" menu item has a nested unordered list, creating a dropdown menu when the user hovers or clicks on it.

Dropdown menus can be styled and made interactive using CSS and JavaScript to enhance the user experience.

Mobile-Friendly Navigation

In today's mobile-centric world, it's crucial to ensure that your navigation menus are responsive and mobile-friendly. You can achieve this by using techniques like media queries to adapt menu styles and structures for smaller screens, or by implementing mobile-specific navigation patterns like the "hamburger" menu.

Summary

Navigation menus are essential for guiding users through your website and providing easy access to various pages or sections. HTML lists, both unordered and ordered, are commonly used to structure navigation menus. CSS can be applied to style and enhance the visual appeal of menus. Dropdown menus are useful for organizing complex site structures, and it's important to make navigation menus mobile-friendly for a seamless user experience.

6.5 Styling Links with CSS

CSS (Cascading Style Sheets) is a powerful tool for styling web content, including hyperlinks. In this section, we'll explore how CSS can be used to style links to make them visually appealing and enhance the user experience.

Basic Link Styles

By default, web browsers apply a basic set of styles to links to distinguish them from regular text. Typically, links are displayed in blue and are underlined. Visited links are usually displayed in purple. However, these default styles can be easily customized using CSS to match the design of your website.

Here's a basic example of CSS rules for styling links:

```css
/* Style unvisited links */
a {
    text-decoration: none; /* Remove underlines */
    color: #0078d4; /* Set link color to blue */
}

/* Style visited links */
a:visited {
    color: #551a8b; /* Set visited link color to purple */
}

/* Style links on hover */
a:hover {
    text-decoration: underline; /* Add underline on hover */
}
```

In this example, we've set the link color to blue for unvisited links, purple for visited links, and added an underline on hover.

Customizing Link Styles

CSS provides a wide range of properties to customize link styles further. Some common properties for link styling include:

- color: Sets the color of the link text.
- text-decoration: Controls the text decoration, which can be used to remove underlines, add underlines, or change other decorations.
- font-weight: Adjusts the thickness or boldness of the text.
- background-color: Sets the background color behind the link text.
- border: Adds borders around the link.
- padding and margin: Control the spacing around the link text.
- display: Specifies how the link is displayed, which can be useful for creating button-like links.

Here's an example that uses some of these properties to style links as buttons:

```css
/* Style links as buttons */
a.button {
    display: inline-block; /* Display as block-level element */
    padding: 10px 20px; /* Add padding around text */
    background-color: #0078d4; /* Set background color */
    color: #ffffff; /* Set text color to white */
    text-decoration: none; /* Remove underlines */
    border: 2px solid #0078d4; /* Add a border */
    border-radius: 5px; /* Add rounded corners */
    font-weight: bold; /* Make text bold */
}

/* Style button links on hover */
```

```css
a.button:hover {
  background-color: #005b9f; /* Change background color on hover */
}
```

With these CSS rules, you can apply the `button` class to your links to style them as buttons.

Pseudo-classes and Pseudo-elements

CSS also provides pseudo-classes and pseudo-elements to target specific states or parts of a link. Some commonly used pseudo-classes for links include:

- `:hover`: Styles the link when the mouse pointer hovers over it.
- `:active`: Styles the link when it is clicked.
- `:focus`: Styles the link when it gains focus (e.g., when using keyboard navigation).

Pseudo-elements, such as `::before` and `::after`, can be used to add content or styling before or after a link, providing additional design possibilities.

Accessibility Considerations

When styling links, it's essential to consider accessibility. Ensure that styled links remain readable and usable for all users, including those with disabilities. Avoid relying solely on color to convey meaning, provide clear visual cues for interactive elements, and test your website with assistive technologies to ensure accessibility compliance.

Summary

CSS offers extensive flexibility for styling links on your website. You can customize link colors, text decorations, fonts, and spacing to match your site's design. Pseudo-classes and pseudo-elements allow you to target specific link states and create interactive effects. While styling links, always keep accessibility in mind to ensure a positive user experience for all visitors.

Chapter 7: Forms and User Input

7.1 Creating HTML Forms

HTML forms are a fundamental part of web development, enabling users to submit data to a web server for various purposes, such as user registration, login, surveys, and more. In this section, we'll delve into the basics of creating HTML forms and the essential elements involved.

The <form> Element

To create a form in HTML, you use the <form> element. The <form> element acts as a container for form controls, including text fields, checkboxes, radio buttons, and buttons. It has several attributes, such as action and method, which define where the form data should be sent and how it should be processed.

Here's a minimal example of an HTML form:

```
<form action="submit.php" method="post">
  <!-- Form controls go here -->
  <label for="username">Username:</label>
  <input type="text" id="username" name="username">
  <br>
  <label for="password">Password:</label>
  <input type="password" id="password" name="password">
  <br>
  <input type="submit" value="Submit">
</form>
```

In this example, we've created a form with two input fields (for username and password) and a submit button. The action attribute specifies the URL to which the form data should be submitted, and the method attribute defines the HTTP method to be used (in this case, POST).

Form Controls

Form controls are the elements within a form that allow users to input data or make selections. Some commonly used form controls include:

- <input>: Represents a wide range of input types, such as text, password, email, and more.
- <textarea>: Allows users to enter multi-line text.
- <select>: Creates a dropdown menu for selecting options.
- <button>: Creates clickable buttons.
- <label>: Provides labels for form controls and improves accessibility.
- <fieldset>: Groups related form controls together.

- `<legend>`: Provides a caption for a `<fieldset>`.

You can specify the type of input or control using the `type` attribute for `<input>` elements.

The name Attribute

Each form control should have a unique `name` attribute, which identifies the control when the form is submitted. The `name` attribute's value is used as the key in the data sent to the server. For example, in the form above, the username field has the `name` attribute set to "username," and the password field has "password."

The `<label>` Element

Using the `<label>` element is good practice because it associates a text label with a form control, making it more accessible and user-friendly. The `for` attribute of the `<label>` should match the `id` of the associated form control. When a user clicks on the label, it focuses on the associated input field.

Submitting Form Data

When a user submits a form, the data entered into the form controls is sent to the server for processing. The server-side processing can be handled using server-side scripting languages like PHP, Python, or JavaScript (Node.js).

In the example form above, when the user clicks the "Submit" button, the data is sent to "submit.php" using the POST method. The server-side script (e.g., PHP) can access the form data using the `name` attributes of the form controls.

Summary

HTML forms are essential for collecting user input and interacting with web servers. They consist of form controls like input fields and buttons enclosed within a `<form>` element. Each form control should have a unique `name` attribute for data identification. Using the `<label>` element improves accessibility and user experience. When users submit a form, the data is sent to a server for processing, often handled by server-side scripting languages. Understanding how to create forms is a crucial skill in web development.

7.2 Form Elements and Attributes

In the previous section, we introduced the basics of creating HTML forms. In this section, we will delve deeper into form elements and attributes, exploring the various input types, attributes, and techniques for building effective forms.

Input Types

HTML offers a variety of input types that cater to different data entry requirements. Here are some commonly used input types:

- **Text**: `<input type="text">` allows users to input single-line text data.
- **Password**: `<input type="password">` is used for entering confidential information like passwords. Characters are usually masked.
- **Email**: `<input type="email">` validates that the input conforms to an email address format.
- **Number**: `<input type="number">` restricts input to numeric values, with optional step and range attributes.
- **Date**: `<input type="date">` is used for selecting a date from a date picker.
- **Checkbox**: `<input type="checkbox">` allows users to select one or more options.
- **Radio Buttons**: `<input type="radio">` is used for exclusive selection within a group.
- **File Upload**: `<input type="file">` lets users upload files to the server.
- **Textarea**: `<textarea>` is used for multi-line text input.
- **Select Menu**: `<select>` creates a dropdown menu with `<option>` elements for selecting an option.
- **Buttons**: `<button>` elements can be used to create buttons for form submission or custom actions.

Each input type serves a specific purpose and can be customized further using attributes.

Common Attributes

Form elements can have various attributes that influence their behavior and appearance. Some commonly used attributes include:

- `name`: Provides a name for the form control, used to identify it when the form is submitted.
- `id`: Assigns a unique identifier to the form control, often associated with a `<label>` element.
- `value`: Specifies the default value for the form control.
- `placeholder`: Provides a hint or example text to guide users.
- `required`: Makes a field mandatory, preventing form submission until it's filled.
- `disabled`: Disables a form control, making it non-editable.
- `readonly`: Makes a form control read-only, allowing viewing but not editing.
- `min and max`: Defines the minimum and maximum values for numeric inputs.
- `step`: Specifies the increment value for numeric inputs.
- `multiple`: Allows multiple selections for file uploads and select menus.
- `autofocus`: Automatically focuses on the form control when the page loads.

Grouping Form Controls

To create logical groupings of form controls, you can use the `<fieldset>` and `<legend>` elements. The `<fieldset>` element groups related form controls together, while the `<legend>` element provides a caption or description for the group. This improves accessibility and organizes the form.

```
<fieldset>
  <legend>Contact Information</legend>
  <!-- Form controls related to contact information go here -->
</fieldset>
```

Form Validation

Form validation ensures that the data entered by users conforms to specified criteria before submission. HTML5 introduced built-in form validation using attributes like `required`, `type`, `min`, `max`, and `pattern`. Additionally, JavaScript can be used for custom validation, providing a more robust solution.

```
<input type="email" name="email" id="email" required>
```

In this example, the `type` attribute specifies that the input should be an email address, and the `required` attribute makes it mandatory.

Summary

Form elements and attributes are crucial for building interactive and user-friendly web forms. By choosing the right input types, using attributes effectively, and organizing form controls logically, you can create forms that collect and validate data efficiently. Understanding form validation techniques, both in HTML and JavaScript, is essential for creating robust and user-friendly web forms.

7.3 Form Validation

Form validation is a crucial aspect of web development that ensures the data submitted by users adheres to specific criteria and is accurate before it is processed by the server. Proper validation enhances user experience and helps maintain data integrity. In this section, we'll explore various methods of form validation in HTML.

Built-In HTML5 Validation

HTML5 introduced built-in form validation attributes that simplify the process of validating user input. These attributes are applied directly to form controls and help enforce data requirements without the need for custom JavaScript code.

required

The `required` attribute is used to specify that a form field must be filled out before submitting the form. It ensures that the field is not left empty.

```
<input type="text" name="username" required>
```

type

The `type` attribute is used to specify the expected format of the input data. For example, using `type="email"` on an input field ensures that the entered value is a valid email address.

```
<input type="email" name="email" required>
```

min and max

For numeric inputs, you can use the `min` and `max` attributes to define acceptable value ranges. For example, you can restrict an input to values between 1 and 100.

```
<input type="number" name="age" min="1" max="100">
```

pattern

The `pattern` attribute allows you to specify a regular expression pattern that the input must match. This provides flexibility in validating complex input patterns, such as phone numbers or postal codes.

```
<input type="text" name="phone" pattern="[0-9]{10}" placeholder="Enter 10-digit phone number">
```

Custom Error Messages

You can customize the error messages displayed to users when validation fails by using the `setCustomValidity` method in JavaScript. This allows you to provide more user-friendly error messages.

```
<input type="text" name="username" required oninvalid="this.setCustomValidity('Please enter your username.')">
```

JavaScript Validation

While built-in HTML5 validation is convenient for simple cases, more complex validation requirements may necessitate custom JavaScript validation. JavaScript validation provides greater flexibility and control over the validation process.

You can use JavaScript event listeners, such as `onsubmit`, `oninput`, or `onblur`, to trigger validation functions. These functions can check form field values, perform custom validation logic, and display error messages dynamically.

```
<form onsubmit="return validateForm()">
  <input type="text" name="username" id="username">
  <span id="username-error" class="error"></span>
  <input type="submit" value="Submit">
</form>

<script>
  function validateForm() {
    var username = document.getElementById("username").value;
```

```
    var errorElement = document.getElementById("username-error");

    if (username.length < 5) {
      errorElement.textContent = "Username must be at least 5 characters long
.";
      return false;
    }

    // Additional custom validation logic here

    return true; // Form is valid
  }
</script>
```

In this example, the validateForm JavaScript function checks the length of the username input and displays an error message if it's too short.

Summary

Form validation is essential to ensure data accuracy and enhance user experience. HTML5 provides built-in validation attributes like required, type, min, and max for simple validation tasks. For more complex validation requirements, custom JavaScript validation can be implemented using event listeners and validation functions. Combining both approaches can provide a robust validation solution for your web forms.

7.4 Handling Form Submissions

Handling form submissions is a critical part of web development, as it involves processing and validating user input on the server-side. In this section, we'll explore how to handle form submissions using HTML and server-side scripting languages like PHP.

Form Submission Basics

When a user submits a form on a web page, the data entered into the form fields is sent to the server for processing. The server-side script specified in the form's action attribute receives this data and can perform various actions, such as storing it in a database, sending emails, or generating dynamic content.

Here's a simple HTML form that submits data to a PHP script:

```
<form action="process.php" method="post">
  <label for="name">Name:</label>
  <input type="text" name="name" id="name">
  <input type="submit" value="Submit">
</form>
```

In this example, when the user clicks the "Submit" button, the form data is sent to the "process.php" script using the POST method.

Server-Side Scripting

Server-side scripting languages like PHP, Python, Ruby, and Node.js are commonly used to handle form submissions. In this section, we'll focus on PHP as an example.

PHP Script (process.php)

```php
<?php
if ($_SERVER["REQUEST_METHOD"] == "POST") {
  $name = $_POST["name"];
  // Perform server-side validation and processing here
  echo "Hello, $name! Your form has been submitted.";
} else {
  // Handle other request methods or direct URL access
  echo "Invalid request.";
}
?>
```

In the PHP script above, we check if the request method is POST using `$_SERVER["REQUEST_METHOD"]`. If it is, we retrieve the submitted "name" field value from `$_POST` and perform any necessary validation and processing. Finally, we generate a response, which is sent back to the web page for display.

Form Data Retrieval

To access form data on the server-side, you use the `$_POST` superglobal in PHP. The keys of `$_POST` correspond to the "name" attributes of the form fields. You can retrieve, validate, and sanitize the data as needed for your application.

Validation and Security

Proper validation and security measures are crucial when handling form submissions. Always validate and sanitize user input to prevent security vulnerabilities like SQL injection and cross-site scripting (XSS) attacks. Additionally, validate form data for correctness (e.g., email format, required fields) and handle errors gracefully.

Redirecting After Submission

After processing a form submission, it's a good practice to redirect the user to another page to avoid resubmission if they refresh the page. You can use the PHP `header` function to achieve this.

```php
header("Location: thank-you.php");
exit; // Ensure no further code execution
```

Summary

Handling form submissions involves collecting and processing user input on the server-side. HTML forms send data to a server-side script specified in the form's `action` attribute. Server-side scripting languages like PHP are commonly used to process form data, validate it, and generate responses. Proper validation, security measures, and redirection after submission are essential considerations when implementing form handling in web applications.

7.5 Advanced Form Features

While basic form elements cover many use cases, there are advanced form features and techniques that can enhance the functionality and user experience of web forms. In this section, we'll explore some of these advanced form features.

1. Form Validation with JavaScript

While HTML5 provides built-in form validation attributes like `required` and `pattern`, JavaScript can be used to implement more complex and custom validation logic. By attaching event listeners to form fields and using JavaScript functions, you can create dynamic and responsive validation.

Here's an example of using JavaScript to validate a password field for complexity:

```html
<input type="password" name="password" id="password" required>
<span id="password-error" class="error"></span>

<script>
  const passwordField = document.getElementById("password");
  const passwordError = document.getElementById("password-error");

  passwordField.addEventListener("input", function () {
    const password = passwordField.value;
    if (password.length < 8) {
      passwordError.textContent = "Password must be at least 8 characters long.";
    } else {
      passwordError.textContent = "";
    }
  });
</script>
```

2. Conditional Fields

Conditional fields allow you to show or hide form elements based on user input. This can be useful for creating dynamic forms where certain fields become relevant only when specific conditions are met. JavaScript is often used to implement conditional field behavior.

```html
<input type="radio" name="membership" value="yes"> Yes
<input type="radio" name="membership" value="no"> No

<div id="membership-details" style="display: none;">
  <input type="text" name="membership-number" placeholder="Membership Number"
```

```
>
</div>

<script>
  const membershipRadio = document.querySelectorAll('input[name="membership"]
');
  const membershipDetails = document.getElementById("membership-details");

  membershipRadio.forEach((radio) => {
    radio.addEventListener("change", function () {
      if (radio.value === "yes") {
        membershipDetails.style.display = "block";
      } else {
        membershipDetails.style.display = "none";
      }
    });
  });
</script>
```

In this example, the "Membership Number" field is displayed or hidden based on the user's selection of "Yes" or "No" for membership.

3. Auto-Suggestions and Auto-Complete

Auto-suggestions and auto-complete features enhance user input by providing suggestions or completing input based on previous entries or data sources. These features are often implemented using JavaScript libraries or frameworks and are commonly used in search boxes and address fields.

4. Multi-Step Forms

Multi-step forms break long or complex forms into smaller, more manageable sections, making it easier for users to navigate and complete the form. JavaScript is used to control the progression through the steps.

5. File Upload Progress

When handling file uploads, it's helpful to provide feedback on the upload progress. JavaScript and server-side code can be used to implement file upload progress indicators.

6. Accessible Forms

Creating accessible forms is essential to ensure that all users, including those with disabilities, can interact with and submit forms. Using semantic HTML elements, providing proper labels, and using ARIA attributes for accessibility are crucial considerations.

Summary

Advanced form features and techniques allow you to create more interactive and user-friendly web forms. These features include custom form validation with JavaScript, conditional fields, auto-suggestions, multi-step forms, file upload progress indicators, and accessibility considerations. By leveraging these advanced techniques, you can improve the user experience and collect data more efficiently in your web applications.

Chapter 8: Tables for Data Organization

8.1 Creating HTML Tables

HTML tables are a powerful tool for organizing and displaying data in a structured format. In this section, we'll explore how to create HTML tables, define their structure, and add data to them.

Basic Table Structure

An HTML table is constructed using several elements, with the most fundamental ones being <table>, <tr>, <th>, and <td>.

- <table>: This is the container element for the entire table.
- <tr>: Stands for "table row" and is used to define a row within the table.
- <th>: Stands for "table header" and is used to define header cells within a row. Header cells are typically bold and centered.
- <td>: Stands for "table data" and is used to define data cells within a row.

Here's an example of a basic HTML table structure:

```
<table>
  <tr>
    <th>Header 1</th>
    <th>Header 2</th>
    <th>Header 3</th>
  </tr>
  <tr>
    <td>Data 1</td>
    <td>Data 2</td>
    <td>Data 3</td>
  </tr>
  <tr>
    <td>Data 4</td>
    <td>Data 5</td>
    <td>Data 6</td>
  </tr>
</table>
```

Table Headers

In the example above, we used <th> elements to define table headers. Headers provide context for the data in each column. It's a best practice to use headers in your tables to improve accessibility and clarify the table's content.

Table Borders and Styling

By default, HTML tables have borders around cells and rows. You can control the appearance of table borders using CSS. Here's an example of CSS to remove table borders and add some basic styling:

```
<style>
  table {
    border-collapse: collapse;
    width: 100%;
  }
  th, td {
    border: 1px solid #dddddd;
    text-align: left;
    padding: 8px;
  }
  tr:nth-child(even) {
    background-color: #f2f2f2;
  }
</style>
```

Table Captions

You can add a caption to your table using the <caption> element. Captions provide a title or description for the table and are usually placed above the table.

```
<table>
  <caption>Monthly Sales Report</caption>
  <!-- Table content here -->
</table>
```

Spanning Rows and Columns

Sometimes, you may need to span rows or columns to create more complex table structures. You can use the rowspan and colspan attributes to achieve this. For example:

```
<table>
  <tr>
    <th rowspan="2">Header 1</th>
    <th>Header 2</th>
  </tr>
  <tr>
    <td>Data 1</td>
  </tr>
</table>
```

In this example, the first header cell spans two rows.

Summary

HTML tables are a versatile tool for organizing and displaying tabular data. You can define table structure using elements like <table>, <tr>, <th>, and <td>, and you can style tables using CSS. Table headers provide context, captions offer descriptions, and spanning rows and columns allow for more complex layouts. Understanding how to create and style tables is valuable for presenting data effectively on your web pages.

8.2 Table Structure and Elements

In the previous section, we discussed the basic structure of HTML tables and how to create them. Now, let's dive deeper into the various elements and attributes you can use to define the structure and appearance of tables.

Table Sections

HTML tables can be divided into several sections for better organization and styling. The main sections of a table are:

- <thead>: This section contains the table header rows (usually the first row or rows) that define column headers.
- <tbody>: This section contains the table's body, where the main data is placed.
- <tfoot>: This section contains the table footer rows (usually the last row or rows) that provide summaries or totals.

Here's an example of how to structure a table using these sections:

```
<table>
  <thead>
    <tr>
      <th>Product ID</th>
      <th>Product Name</th>
      <th>Price</th>
    </tr>
  </thead>
  <tbody>
    <tr>
      <td>101</td>
      <td>Product A</td>
      <td>$20.00</td>
    </tr>
    <tr>
      <td>102</td>
      <td>Product B</td>
      <td>$25.00</td>
    </tr>
  </tbody>
  <tfoot>
```

```
    <tr>
      <td colspan="2">Total:</td>
      <td>$45.00</td>
    </tr>
  </tfoot>
</table>
```

Table Headers and Cells

Within each table section, you can use the <th> element for header cells and the <td> element for data cells. Header cells are typically bold and centered by default, while data cells are left-aligned.

```
<table>
  <thead>
    <tr>
      <th>Header 1</th>
      <th>Header 2</th>
    </tr>
  </thead>
  <tbody>
    <tr>
      <td>Data 1</td>
      <td>Data 2</td>
    </tr>
  </tbody>
</table>
```

Table Row Grouping

To group rows within a table section, you can use the <tr> element. Grouping rows is useful when you want to apply styling or structure to specific rows.

```
<table>
  <tbody>
    <tr>
      <td>Data A</td>
      <td>Data B</td>
    </tr>
    <!-- Group of rows with a common attribute -->
    <tr class="highlighted">
      <td>Data C</td>
      <td>Data D</td>
    </tr>
    <tr class="highlighted">
      <td>Data E</td>
      <td>Data F</td>
    </tr>
    <tr>
      <td>Data G</td>
      <td>Data H</td>
```

```
    </tr>
  </tbody>
</table>
```

In this example, rows with the "highlighted" class are grouped together.

Summary

Understanding the various elements and attributes available for structuring HTML tables is essential for creating well-organized and styled tables. You can use table sections like <thead>, <tbody>, and <tfoot> for better organization, <th> and <td> elements for defining header and data cells, and grouping rows with common attributes for styling and structuring purposes. Properly structured tables improve data presentation and accessibility on web pages.

8.3 Styling Tables with CSS

Once you have created the basic structure of your HTML table, you can enhance its appearance and layout using Cascading Style Sheets (CSS). CSS provides a wide range of styling options for tables, allowing you to customize borders, spacing, colors, and more. In this section, we'll explore some common techniques for styling HTML tables with CSS.

1. Table Borders and Padding

You can control the border and padding of table elements (such as <th> and <td>) using CSS properties like border, border-collapse, and padding. For example, to remove borders and add padding to table cells, you can use the following CSS:

```css
table {
    border-collapse: collapse; /* Remove cell spacing */
}

th, td {
    border: 1px solid #ddd; /* Add borders to cells */
    padding: 8px; /* Add padding inside cells */
}
```

2. Table Background Colors

You can set background colors for table elements to improve visual distinction. Use the background-color property to specify colors for headers, data cells, or even rows:

```css
th {
    background-color: #f2f2f2; /* Light gray background for headers */
}

tr:nth-child(odd) {
```

```
  background-color: #f5f5f5; /* Alternate row background color */
}
```

3. Text Alignment

To align text within table cells, use the `text-align` property. For example, to center-align header text:

```
th {
  text-align: center;
}
```

4. Hover Effects

You can add hover effects to table rows to provide visual feedback when users interact with the table. Here's an example of changing the background color when hovering over rows:

```
tr:hover {
  background-color: #e0e0e0; /* Light gray background on hover */
}
```

5. Borders and Styling for Specific Columns

You can apply specific styling to individual columns by adding classes to `<th>` and `<td>` elements or by using CSS selectors. For instance, to add a border to the first column:

```
th.first-column, td.first-column {
  border-left: 2px solid #333; /* Left border for the first column */
}
```

6. Responsive Tables

To make tables responsive on smaller screens, you can use CSS media queries to adjust their layout. One common technique is to make the table scroll horizontally on narrow screens:

```
@media (max-width: 768px) {
  table {
    width: 100%;
    overflow-x: auto;
  }
}
```

This allows users to scroll horizontally to view the table's content on smaller screens.

7. CSS Frameworks

Consider using CSS frameworks like Bootstrap or Bulma, which provide pre-designed table styles and classes. These frameworks can save you time and offer consistent styling across your web application.

Styling HTML tables with CSS not only improves their visual appeal but also enhances readability and user experience. Experiment with different CSS properties to achieve the desired look and feel for your tables while keeping them accessible and responsive.

8.4 Table Accessibility

Accessibility is a crucial aspect of web development. Making your HTML tables accessible ensures that all users, including those with disabilities, can understand and interact with the content effectively. In this section, we'll explore key accessibility considerations for HTML tables.

1. Use Semantic HTML

Start by using semantic HTML elements appropriately. Use `<table>` for tabular data, `<thead>`, `<tbody>`, and `<tfoot>` for organizing sections, `<th>` for headers, and `<td>` for data cells. Semantic elements help assistive technologies interpret the table's structure correctly.

2. Add Table Captions

Include a `<caption>` element inside your `<table>` to provide a brief and meaningful description of the table's content. Captions assist screen readers in conveying the table's purpose to users.

```
<table>
  <caption>Monthly Expenses</caption>
  <!-- Table content -->
</table>
```

3. Use Header Cells

Use `<th>` elements for table headers. Each data cell (`<td>`) within a column should have a corresponding header cell (`<th>`) in the same column. This association helps screen readers and users understand the relationship between headers and data.

```
<table>
  <thead>
    <tr>
      <th>Product ID</th>
      <th>Product Name</th>
      <th>Price</th>
    </tr>
  </thead>
  <tbody>
    <tr>
      <td>101</td>
      <td>Product A</td>
      <td>$20.00</td>
```

```
    </tr>
    <!-- More rows -->
  </tbody>
</table>
```

4. Use Scope and Headers Attributes

To associate header cells with data cells explicitly, use the scope and headers attributes. The scope attribute specifies whether a header cell applies to a column or row, while the headers attribute lists the IDs of associated header cells.

```
<table>
  <thead>
    <tr>
      <th scope="col" id="product-id-header">Product ID</th>
      <th scope="col" id="product-name-header">Product Name</th>
      <th scope="col" id="price-header">Price</th>
    </tr>
  </thead>
  <tbody>
    <tr>
      <td headers="product-id-header">101</td>
      <td headers="product-name-header">Product A</td>
      <td headers="price-header">$20.00</td>
    </tr>
    <!-- More rows -->
  </tbody>
</table>
```

5. Provide Table Summaries

For complex tables, consider including a summary attribute that provides a concise overview of the table's content and purpose. This is especially helpful for users with disabilities.

```
<table summary="This table displays monthly expenses for various categories."
>
  <!-- Table content -->
</table>
```

6. Test with Screen Readers

To ensure accessibility, test your tables with screen reader software like NVDA, JAWS, or VoiceOver. Navigate through the table content to verify that headers are announced correctly and that the table is understandable.

7. Keyboard Navigation

Ensure that your table is navigable using a keyboard. Users should be able to navigate between cells and hear headers when moving through rows and columns. Use the tabindex attribute to control the tab order.

Creating accessible tables is a critical part of web development. By following these best practices, you can make your tables inclusive and usable by all individuals, regardless of their abilities or assistive technologies.

8.5 Responsive Tables

In today's web development landscape, responsive design is paramount. A responsive table is one that adapts to different screen sizes and devices, ensuring that the table remains usable and readable on small screens like smartphones and tablets. In this section, we'll explore techniques for creating responsive tables in HTML and CSS.

1. Horizontal Scrolling

One common approach to handle wide tables on small screens is to allow horizontal scrolling. You can achieve this by wrapping the table in a container with an `overflow-x: auto;` style rule. This allows users to scroll horizontally to view the entire table.

```
<div class="table-container">
  <table>
    <!-- Table content -->
  </table>
</div>

.table-container {
  overflow-x: auto;
}
```

2. Hide Columns

For extremely wide tables, consider hiding less important columns on smaller screens. You can use CSS media queries to hide specific columns based on screen width. Here's an example of hiding a column with a class of `hide-on-mobile` on screens smaller than 768 pixels:

```
@media (max-width: 768px) {
  .hide-on-mobile {
    display: none;
  }
}

<table>
  <tr>
    <th class="hide-on-mobile">Column 1</th>
    <th>Column 2</th>
    <!-- ... -->
  </tr>
  <!-- Table content -->
</table>
```

3. Stack Rows

For narrow screens, consider stacking rows vertically instead of displaying them in a traditional table format. Each row becomes a separate block element, making it easier to read on small screens.

```css
@media (max-width: 768px) {
  table {
    display: block;
  }
  tr {
    display: block;
    margin-bottom: 20px;
  }
}
```

4. Responsive Tables with CSS Frameworks

Many CSS frameworks, like Bootstrap, come with built-in classes for creating responsive tables. These classes automatically handle various responsive table behaviors, such as horizontal scrolling and column hiding, without requiring custom CSS.

5. Testing on Multiple Devices

Always test your responsive tables on a variety of devices and screen sizes to ensure they function as intended. Use browser developer tools to simulate different screen sizes during development.

6. Consider Mobile-First Design

Adopting a mobile-first design approach means creating your table's initial layout for mobile devices and then progressively enhancing it for larger screens. This approach ensures that the table is usable on all devices from the start.

Responsive tables play a vital role in providing a positive user experience on mobile devices. By implementing these techniques, you can make your tables adapt to various screen sizes, ensuring that your content remains accessible and user-friendly regardless of the device being used.

Chapter 9: Semantic HTML5 Elements

Semantic HTML5 elements are a fundamental part of modern web development. They provide a way to structure web content in a meaningful and machine-readable manner. In this chapter, we'll explore the importance of semantic elements and how to use them effectively.

9.1 Understanding Semantic Markup

Semantic HTML, also known as semantic markup, involves using HTML elements that convey meaning about the structure and content of a web page. This approach makes it easier for both humans and search engines to understand the purpose and hierarchy of the page's content. Let's delve into the key concepts of semantic markup.

1. The Role of Semantic Elements

Semantic elements are HTML tags that carry inherent meaning. Examples include `<header>`, `<nav>`, `<main>`, `<article>`, `<section>`, `<aside>`, and `<footer>`. These elements describe the type of content they contain and its relationship to the rest of the page.

```html
<header>
  <h1>My Website</h1>
  <nav>
    <!-- Navigation links -->
  </nav>
</header>
<main>
  <article>
    <!-- Article content -->
  </article>
  <aside>
    <!-- Sidebar content -->
  </aside>
</main>
<footer>
  <!-- Footer content -->
</footer>
```

2. Benefits of Semantic Markup

Semantic HTML offers several advantages:

- **Accessibility:** Semantic elements provide a clearer structure for screen readers and assistive technologies, improving accessibility.
- **SEO:** Search engines can better understand the content and context of your page, potentially leading to better search rankings.

- **Readability:** Semantic markup enhances the readability of your code, making it easier to maintain and collaborate on.

3. Common Semantic Elements

- `<header>`: Represents a container for introductory content or a set of navigational links.
- `<nav>`: Defines a section with navigation links.
- `<main>`: Represents the primary content of the document.
- `<article>`: Defines self-contained content that could be distributed and reused independently.
- `<section>`: Groups related content together and typically has its own heading.
- `<aside>`: Represents content that is tangentially related to the content around it.
- `<footer>`: Defines the footer of a section or page.

4. Using Semantic Elements

When structuring a web page, think about the meaning and purpose of the content. Choose semantic elements that accurately describe the content's role and relationship to other elements. Use headings (`<h1>` to `<h6>`) to establish a hierarchy within sections and articles.

```
<article>
  <h1>How to Bake a Perfect Cake</h1>
  <p>...article content...</p>
  <section>
    <h2>Ingredients</h2>
    <ul>
      <!-- Ingredient List -->
    </ul>
  </section>
  <section>
    <h2>Instructions</h2>
    <ol>
      <!-- Step-by-step instructions -->
    </ol>
  </section>
</article>
```

5. Fallback for Older Browsers

While modern browsers fully support semantic elements, it's essential to provide a fallback for older browsers that may not recognize them. This can be achieved by using CSS for styling and JavaScript for adding missing elements if necessary.

Semantic HTML5 elements are a cornerstone of web development. By using them effectively, you can create web pages that are more accessible, readable, and search engine-friendly. In the following sections, we'll explore specific semantic elements in more detail and see how they can be applied to various types of content.

9.2 HTML5 Structural Elements

HTML5 introduced a set of structural elements that provide a more meaningful way to define the layout and organization of web documents. These elements help developers create well-structured, semantic web pages. In this section, we'll delve into HTML5 structural elements and their usage.

1. `<header>`

The `<header>` element represents a container for introductory content or a set of navigational links. It typically includes elements like headings, logos, and navigation menus. This element is often placed at the top of a page or within a `<section>` to mark its beginning.

```html
<header>
  <h1>My Website</h1>
  <nav>
    <ul>
      <li><a href="/">Home</a></li>
      <li><a href="/about">About</a></li>
      <li><a href="/contact">Contact</a></li>
    </ul>
  </nav>
</header>
```

2. `<nav>`

The `<nav>` element defines a section with navigation links. It's typically used to group links that allow users to navigate between different parts of a website. This element is commonly found within the `<header>` or as part of a site's footer.

```html
<nav>
  <ul>
    <li><a href="/">Home</a></li>
    <li><a href="/products">Products</a></li>
    <li><a href="/services">Services</a></li>
    <li><a href="/contact">Contact</a></li>
  </ul>
</nav>
```

3. `<main>`

The `<main>` element represents the primary content of the document. It should contain the main content that is unique to the page and is not repeated across multiple pages. There should be only one `<main>` element per page.

```html
<main>
  <h1>Latest News</h1>
```

```
<article>
  <!-- Article content goes here -->
</article>
</main>
```

4. <article>

The `<article>` element defines self-contained content that could be distributed and reused independently. It's commonly used for blog posts, news articles, forum posts, and similar content. Each `<article>` should have a heading that describes its content.

```
<article>
  <h2>How to Start a Blog</h2>
  <p>...article content...</p>
</article>
```

5. <section>

The `<section>` element is used to group related content together and typically has its own heading. It helps to divide the content into meaningful sections, making it easier to understand the page's structure.

```
<section>
  <h2>About Us</h2>
  <p>We are a team of passionate individuals...</p>
</section>
```

6. <aside>

The `<aside>` element represents content that is tangentially related to the content around it. It's often used for sidebars, pull quotes, advertising, or other content that complements the main content.

```
<aside>
  <h3>Related Links</h3>
  <ul>
    <li><a href="/related-article-1">Related Article 1</a></li>
    <li><a href="/related-article-2">Related Article 2</a></li>
  </ul>
</aside>
```

7. <footer>

The `<footer>` element defines the footer of a section or the entire page. It typically contains copyright information, contact details, and links to related pages or resources.

```
<footer>
  <p>&copy; 2023 My Website</p>
  <p>Contact: contact@mywebsite.com</p>
</footer>
```

These HTML5 structural elements provide a more semantic way to structure web documents, making them more accessible and understandable. By using these elements effectively, you can improve the overall quality of your web pages and enhance their compatibility with assistive technologies and search engines.

9.3 Using Header and Footer Elements

In HTML5, the `<header>` and `<footer>` elements serve specific roles in structuring web content. In this section, we'll explore how to use these elements effectively to provide additional context and information to web pages.

1. The `<header>` Element

The `<header>` element represents a container for introductory content or a set of navigational links that appear at the top of a section or page. While it's commonly used at the top of a webpage within the `<body>` element, it can also be used within other structural elements like `<article>` or `<section>` to define headers for those sections.

Basic Usage

```
<header>
  <h1>Welcome to My Website</h1>
  <nav>
    <ul>
      <li><a href="/">Home</a></li>
      <li><a href="/about">About Us</a></li>
      <li><a href="/contact">Contact</a></li>
    </ul>
  </nav>
</header>
```

In this example, the `<header>` contains a heading `<h1>` and a navigation menu. It provides essential introductory content and navigation options for the webpage.

`<header>` Within Sections

You can also use the `<header>` element within `<section>` elements to provide context for those sections. For example:

```
<section>
  <header>
    <h2>About Us</h2>
  </header>
  <p>We are a passionate team dedicated to...</p>
</section>
```

This usage of `<header>` helps define the header for the "About Us" section.

2. The `<footer>` Element

The `<footer>` element defines the footer of a section or the entire webpage. It typically contains information like copyright notices, contact details, and links to related resources. Similar to `<header>`, it can be used both at the page level and within individual sections.

Basic Usage

```
<footer>
    <p>&copy; 2023 My Website</p>
    <p>Contact: contact@mywebsite.com</p>
</footer>
```

In this example, the `<footer>` contains copyright information and contact details.

`<footer>` Within Sections

Using `<footer>` within sections can help provide context-specific footer content. For instance:

```
<section>
    <h2>Latest News</h2>
    <!-- News articles go here -->
    <footer>
        <p><a href="/news-archive">View All News</a></p>
    </footer>
</section>
```

Here, the `<footer>` within the "Latest News" section contains a link to view all news articles, which is contextually relevant to the section's content.

Semantic Benefits

Using `<header>` and `<footer>` elements in your HTML documents enhances the semantic structure of your web pages. It helps browsers, search engines, and assistive technologies understand the role and context of these elements, ultimately improving accessibility and search engine optimization (SEO).

By incorporating `<header>` and `<footer>` elements appropriately, you can create well-structured web pages that are easier to navigate, understand, and maintain. These elements contribute to a more accessible and user-friendly web experience.

9.4 Semantic Tags for Content

In HTML5, semantic elements play a crucial role in enhancing the structure and meaning of web content. Semantic tags provide information about the type and purpose of the content they enclose, making it easier for both browsers and assistive technologies to understand and interpret web pages correctly. In this section, we'll explore some of the most commonly used semantic tags.

1. `<article>`

The `<article>` element represents a self-contained piece of content that can be distributed and reused independently. It is often used for blog posts, news articles, forum posts, and similar content. Each `<article>` should have a heading that describes its content.

```html
<article>
  <h2>How to Start a Blog</h2>
  <p>Creating a blog is a great way to share your ideas...</p>
</article>
```

2. `<section>`

The `<section>` element is used to group related content together and typically has its own heading. It helps to divide the content into meaningful sections, making it easier to understand the page's structure.

```html
<section>
  <h2>About Us</h2>
  <p>We are a team of passionate individuals...</p>
</section>
```

3. `<aside>`

The `<aside>` element represents content that is tangentially related to the content around it. It's often used for sidebars, pull quotes, advertising, or other content that complements the main content.

```html
<aside>
  <h3>Related Links</h3>
  <ul>
    <li><a href="/related-article-1">Related Article 1</a></li>
    <li><a href="/related-article-2">Related Article 2</a></li>
  </ul>
</aside>
```

4. `<details>` and `<summary>`

The `<details>` and `<summary>` elements are used to create interactive disclosure widgets. `<details>` contains additional content that can be hidden or shown, while `<summary>` provides the initial text or label for the widget.

```html
<details>
  <summary>Click to reveal more information</summary>
  <p>Here's some additional content that can be hidden or shown...</p>
</details>
```

5. `<figure>` and `<figcaption>`

The `<figure>` element is used to encapsulate media content like images, videos, or diagrams, along with an optional `<figcaption>` element that provides a caption for the media.

```
<figure>
  <img src="image.jpg" alt="A beautiful sunset">
  <figcaption>A beautiful sunset over the mountains.</figcaption>
</figure>
```

6. `<mark>`

The `<mark>` element is used to highlight or mark a portion of text within a larger block of content. It's commonly used for highlighting search results.

```
<p>In this passage, the author discusses the <mark>impact of climate change</mark> on wildlife.</p>
```

7. `<time>`

The `<time>` element is used to represent a specific point in time or a duration. It can be especially helpful for marking up dates and times on web pages.

```
<p>Our next event is scheduled for <time datetime="2023-11-15T19:30">November 15, 2023, at 7:30 PM</time>.</p>
```

By incorporating these semantic tags into your HTML markup, you provide valuable context and meaning to your web content. This not only benefits users but also improves the accessibility and SEO of your web pages. Semantically well-structured content is easier for search engines to index and rank, ultimately enhancing the visibility of your website in search results.

9.5 ARIA Roles for Accessibility

ARIA (Accessible Rich Internet Applications) roles are a set of attributes that can be added to HTML elements to enhance the accessibility of web content, particularly for users with disabilities. ARIA roles provide additional information to assistive technologies, such as screen readers, in understanding the purpose and behavior of elements on a web page. In this section, we'll explore some common ARIA roles and how to use them effectively.

1. `role="banner"`

The `role="banner"` attribute is typically used to define the main banner or header section of a web page. It helps screen readers identify and navigate to the primary content of a page, which is often found at the top.

```
<header role="banner">
  <h1>Welcome to Our Website</h1>
```

```
<nav>
  <ul>
    <li><a href="/">Home</a></li>
    <li><a href="/about">About Us</a></li>
    <li><a href="/contact">Contact</a></li>
  </ul>
</nav>
</header>
```

2. role="navigation"

The `role="navigation"` attribute is used to define a navigation menu or menu bar. It helps screen readers identify and navigate to the navigation elements on a page.

```
<nav role="navigation">
  <ul>
    <li><a href="/">Home</a></li>
    <li><a href="/about">About Us</a></li>
    <li><a href="/contact">Contact</a></li>
  </ul>
</nav>
```

3. role="main"

The `role="main"` attribute indicates the main content area of a web page. It assists screen readers in recognizing the central content that users should focus on.

```
<main role="main">
  <h1>Latest News</h1>
  <!-- News articles go here -->
</main>
```

4. role="complementary"

The `role="complementary"` attribute is used for content that complements the main content but is not essential. It helps screen readers distinguish content that provides additional context or information.

```
<aside role="complementary">
  <h3>Related Links</h3>
  <ul>
    <li><a href="/related-article-1">Related Article 1</a></li>
    <li><a href="/related-article-2">Related Article 2</a></li>
  </ul>
</aside>
```

5. role="form"

The `role="form"` attribute is used to define a form element on a web page. It assists screen readers in identifying and navigating form controls.

```
<form role="form" action="/submit" method="post">
  <!-- Form controls go here -->
</form>
```

6. role="button"

The `role="button"` attribute is applied to elements that act as buttons, such as clickable divs or spans. It helps screen readers recognize interactive elements.

```
<div role="button" tabindex="0">Click me</div>
```

7. aria-label and aria-labelledby

In addition to ARIA roles, you can use `aria-label` and `aria-labelledby` attributes to provide descriptive labels for elements that may not have visible text. These attributes can improve the accessibility of icons, images, and other non-text elements.

```
<button aria-label="Close" onclick="closeModal()">&times;</button>
```

When using ARIA roles and attributes, it's important to do so judiciously and accurately. Misuse can lead to confusion rather than improving accessibility. Testing with assistive technologies and following accessibility guidelines is essential to ensure that ARIA enhancements are effective in providing a better user experience for all web visitors.

Chapter 10: Multimedia and Embedding

10.1 Embedding Videos from YouTube

In the ever-evolving landscape of web content, multimedia elements such as videos play a crucial role in engaging users and delivering information. One popular platform for hosting and sharing videos is YouTube. Embedding YouTube videos into your web pages allows you to provide dynamic and interactive content to your audience. In this section, we'll explore how to embed YouTube videos using HTML.

1. Obtaining the YouTube Video URL

Before you can embed a YouTube video, you need to obtain its URL. Visit the YouTube website, locate the video you want to embed, and click on it to open the video page. Then, copy the URL from your web browser's address bar.

2. Embedding with the <iframe> Element

The most common method to embed YouTube videos is by using the <iframe> (inline frame) HTML element. This element allows you to embed external content, such as videos, within your web page. Here's the basic structure of an <iframe> tag for embedding a YouTube video:

```
<iframe
  width="560"
  height="315"
  src="https://www.youtube.com/embed/VIDEO_ID"
  frameborder="0"
  allowfullscreen
></iframe>
```

Replace VIDEO_ID with the actual video ID from the YouTube URL you copied earlier. You can also customize the width and height attributes to control the size of the embedded video player.

3. Customizing the Embed Code

YouTube provides additional options to customize the appearance and behavior of the embedded video. These options are appended to the video URL as query parameters. Here are some commonly used parameters:

- autoplay: Automatically plays the video when the page loads.
- controls: Displays video player controls (play, pause, volume, etc.).
- showinfo: Displays video title and uploader information.
- rel: Shows related videos when the video ends.
- modestbranding: Hides the YouTube logo in the player.

Here's an example of an embedded video with custom parameters:

```
<iframe
  width="560"
  height="315"
  src="https://www.youtube.com/embed/VIDEO_ID?autoplay=1&controls=0&showinfo=
0"
  frameborder="0"
  allowfullscreen
></iframe>
```

4. Responsive Embeds

To ensure that your embedded videos are responsive and adapt to different screen sizes, you can use CSS to style the `<iframe>` element. Here's an example of CSS that makes the embedded video responsive:

```
iframe {
  max-width: 100%;
  height: auto;
}
```

With this CSS, the embedded video will resize proportionally to fit the container width, making it suitable for various devices and screen sizes.

5. JavaScript Integration

If you need to interact with the embedded YouTube video programmatically, you can use the YouTube Iframe API, which provides methods and events for controlling and monitoring video playback through JavaScript. This allows you to implement features like custom controls, tracking video progress, or reacting to video events.

In summary, embedding YouTube videos in your web pages is a straightforward process that enhances your content with engaging multimedia. Remember to consider customization options and responsive design to ensure a seamless user experience. Additionally, JavaScript integration can further extend the capabilities of your embedded videos, making them more interactive and dynamic.

10.2 Using iFrames for Embedded Content

In addition to embedding YouTube videos, web developers often use the `<iframe>` (inline frame) element to embed various types of external content within their web pages. An `<iframe>` allows you to display content from another website or source seamlessly within your own page. This section explores the use of `<iframe>` for embedding external content.

1. Basics of the `<iframe>` Element

The `<iframe>` element is a versatile HTML tag that can be used to embed content like web pages, maps, documents, or even other web applications. Here's a basic example of how to use the `<iframe>` element:

```
<iframe src="https://www.example.com"></iframe>
```

In this example, the `src` attribute specifies the source URL of the content you want to embed. The web page at "https://www.example.com" will be displayed within the `<iframe>` on your page.

2. Controlling the Size of the `<iframe>`

You can control the size of the embedded `<iframe>` using the `width` and `height` attributes. For instance, to set the width to 500 pixels and the height to 300 pixels, you can do the following:

```
<iframe src="https://www.example.com" width="500" height="300"></iframe>
```

Alternatively, you can use CSS to style the `<iframe>` for more precise control over its dimensions and appearance.

3. Responsive iFrames

To make embedded `<iframe>` elements responsive and adapt to different screen sizes, you can use CSS. Here's an example of CSS that ensures the `<iframe>` scales proportionally within its container:

```
iframe {
  max-width: 100%;
  height: auto;
}
```

This CSS ensures that the `<iframe>` will never exceed the width of its container and will maintain its aspect ratio.

4. Security Considerations

When embedding content from external sources using `<iframe>`, it's essential to consider security. Ensure that you trust the source you are embedding, as content within an `<iframe>` has access to your webpage's DOM (Document Object Model) and can potentially execute scripts or access sensitive information.

5. Use Cases for `<iframe>`

The `<iframe>` element is useful for various scenarios, including:

- Embedding maps from services like Google Maps.
- Integrating social media widgets (e.g., Twitter, Facebook).
- Displaying documents or PDFs.

- Embedding web applications or forms from third-party providers.

Keep in mind that while `<iframe>` is a powerful tool for embedding external content, it should be used judiciously to maintain a consistent and secure user experience on your website.

In summary, the `<iframe>` element is a versatile tool for embedding external content into your web pages. When used correctly and securely, it allows you to enrich your site with a wide range of content from different sources while maintaining control over its appearance and behavior.

10.3 Creating Interactive Maps

Interactive maps are a valuable addition to many websites, providing users with location-based information and enhancing the overall user experience. In this section, we'll explore how to create and embed interactive maps into your web pages using popular mapping services like Google Maps.

1. Embedding Google Maps

Google Maps offers a straightforward way to embed interactive maps on your website. To get started, follow these steps:

a. Go to the Google Maps website

Visit the Google Maps website and find the location you want to embed.

b. Access the map's menu

Click on the "Menu" icon (usually represented by three horizontal lines) in the top-left corner of the map to open the map's menu.

c. Choose "Share or embed map"

From the menu, select "Share or embed map."

d. Embed the map

In the "Share via" tab, choose the "Embed a map" option.

e. Customize the map

You can customize the map's size by selecting a preset size or entering custom dimensions. You can also choose whether to include a map title, description, and more.

f. Copy the HTML code

Once you've customized the map, Google will generate the HTML code for you. Simply copy the code provided.

Paste the copied HTML code into your webpage's HTML where you want the map to appear.

Here's an example of what the HTML code for embedding a Google Map might look like:

```
<iframe
  src="https://www.google.com/maps/embed?pb=!1m18!1m12!1m3!1d3152.05319374598
2!2d-122.08374068434509!3d37.38605137982985!2m3!1f0!2f0!3f0!3m2!1i1024!2i768!
4f13.1!3m3!1m2!1s0x80859a6d00690021%3A0xe33e18f799f20d19!2sGolden%20Gate%20Br
idge!5e0!3m2!1sen!2sus!4v1598875825299!5m2!1sen!2sus"
  width="600"
  height="450"
  frameborder="0"
  style="border: 0;"
  allowfullscreen=""
  aria-hidden="false"
  tabindex="0"
></iframe>
```

This code embeds a Google Map with specific location coordinates and dimensions.

2. Customizing the Embedded Map

You can further customize the embedded map by adjusting parameters in the `<iframe>` code. For example:

- Modify the `width` and `height` attributes to control the map's size.
- Adjust the `src` URL to specify a different location or customize the map's appearance.
- Include or remove additional options like zoom controls or a map title.

3. Responsive Google Maps

To make your embedded Google Maps responsive and adapt to different screen sizes, you can use CSS to style the `<iframe>` element. Apply styles like `max-width: 100%;` and `height: auto;` to ensure the map scales proportionally within its container.

4. JavaScript Integration

For more advanced functionality, such as adding markers, creating custom map layers, or interacting with the map programmatically, you can use the Google Maps JavaScript API.

In conclusion, embedding interactive maps from services like Google Maps can greatly enhance the user experience on your website, providing valuable location-based information. By following these steps, you can easily integrate maps into your web pages and customize their appearance to suit your needs.

10.4 Working with SVG Graphics

Scalable Vector Graphics (SVG) is a popular format for creating and displaying vector graphics on the web. SVG is a versatile and flexible way to present graphics, ranging from simple icons to complex illustrations. In this section, we'll explore the basics of working with SVG graphics in web development.

1. Understanding SVG

SVG is an XML-based format that describes two-dimensional vector graphics. Unlike raster images (e.g., JPEG or PNG), SVG images are resolution-independent, which means they can be scaled up or down without losing quality. SVG graphics are composed of various shapes, paths, text, and other elements.

2. Creating SVG Images

a. Inline SVG

You can include SVG directly in your HTML document using inline SVG. Here's an example of inline SVG:

```
<svg width="100" height="100" xmlns="http://www.w3.org/2000/svg">
  <circle cx="50" cy="50" r="40" stroke="black" stroke-width="2" fill="red" /
>
</svg>
```

This code creates a red circle inside an SVG container.

b. External SVG

Alternatively, you can save SVG graphics as separate .svg files and include them in your HTML using the <img> tag or the <object> tag.

3. Basic SVG Elements

SVG provides a range of elements to create graphics:

- <rect> for rectangles and squares.
- <circle> for circles.
- <ellipse> for ellipses.
- <line> for straight lines.
- <path> for complex shapes defined by paths.
- <polygon> for closed shapes with multiple sides.
- <polyline> for open shapes with multiple sides.
- <text> for adding text.

4. Styling SVG

You can style SVG elements using CSS, either inline or in an external stylesheet. Use CSS properties like `fill`, `stroke`, `stroke-width`, and `opacity` to control the appearance of SVG elements.

5. Animating SVG

SVG graphics can be animated using CSS animations or JavaScript. You can change attributes like `cx`, `cy`, `r`, or the `d` attribute of a `<path>` element to create animations.

6. Accessibility

Ensure that your SVG graphics are accessible to all users, including those with disabilities. Provide descriptive `<title>` and `<desc>` elements to convey the meaning of the graphic. Use proper text alternatives for non-text content.

7. Compatibility

SVG is well-supported by modern web browsers. However, consider browser compatibility if you need to support older browsers. You can use fallbacks or polyfills if necessary.

8. Optimization

Optimize your SVG files by removing unnecessary elements and attributes to reduce file size. Various online tools and SVG optimization libraries are available to help with this.

9. SVG Libraries and Tools

Several libraries and tools can simplify working with SVG in web development:

- **D3.js:** A powerful library for creating interactive data visualizations with SVG.
- **Snap.svg:** A JavaScript library for working with SVG, making it easier to create and manipulate SVG elements.
- **Inkscape:** A popular open-source vector graphics editor that can export SVG files.
- **SVGOMG:** An online SVG optimization tool.

In conclusion, SVG is a versatile and scalable format for creating vector graphics on the web. Understanding how to create, style, animate, and optimize SVG graphics can add richness and interactivity to your web projects. Incorporating accessibility best practices ensures that all users can benefit from your SVG content.

10.5 Best Practices for Embedded Media

When embedding media such as videos, audio, and interactive content in your web pages, it's essential to follow best practices to ensure a smooth user experience and maintain compatibility across different devices and browsers. In this section, we'll explore some key best practices for working with embedded media.

1. Use Standard HTML5 Elements

For embedding media, HTML5 provides specific elements like <video>, <audio>, and <iframe>. Whenever possible, use these standard HTML5 elements to embed media content. They come with built-in features for accessibility and responsiveness.

```
<!-- Embedding video -->
<video controls width="400" height="300">
  <source src="video.mp4" type="video/mp4">
  Your browser does not support the video tag.
</video>

<!-- Embedding audio -->
<audio controls>
    <source src="audio.mp3" type="audio/mpeg">
    Your browser does not support the audio tag.
</audio>

<!-- Embedding interactive content using iframe -->
<iframe src="https://example.com/interactive-content" width="800" height="600"></iframe>
```

2. Provide Fallback Content

Always include fallback content within the media elements. This content will be displayed if the user's browser does not support the embedded media type. Fallback content can be text or alternative media formats.

3. Implement Accessibility

Make sure your embedded media is accessible to all users. Provide descriptive text alternatives for non-text content using the alt attribute for <img> elements, <track> elements for subtitles and captions in videos, and text transcripts for audio content.

4. Optimize Media

Optimize your media files to reduce their size and improve loading times. Use appropriate formats (e.g., WebM for videos, MP3 for audio) and consider compression to achieve a balance between quality and file size.

5. Ensure Responsiveness

Ensure that embedded media is responsive and adapts to different screen sizes. Use percentage-based dimensions or CSS media queries to adjust the size of media elements based on the device's screen width.

6. Consider Lazy Loading

For large media files, consider implementing lazy loading to defer the loading of media elements until they are visible in the user's viewport. This can significantly improve page load times.

7. Test Cross-Browser Compatibility

Test your embedded media across different browsers and devices to ensure compatibility. Consider using browser-specific prefixes or fallbacks for older browsers that may not support certain media features.

8. Enable Video Autoplay with Caution

Autoplaying videos can be intrusive and affect the user experience negatively. If you decide to autoplay videos, ensure that they don't play with sound by default, as this can be disruptive.

9. Monitor Performance

Regularly monitor the performance of your web pages, especially when embedding media. Use browser developer tools and performance testing tools to identify and address any issues that may impact page load times.

10. Compliance with Copyright

Ensure that you have the necessary permissions and rights to embed and use media content on your website, especially if it's copyrighted material. Always provide proper attribution and adhere to copyright laws and regulations.

By following these best practices, you can enhance the user experience, improve accessibility, and ensure the compatibility and performance of embedded media on your website. This will contribute to a more engaging and user-friendly web presence.

Chapter 11: CSS Basics and Selectors

Section 11.1: Introduction to Cascading Style Sheets

Cascading Style Sheets, commonly referred to as CSS, play a fundamental role in web development. CSS is used to control the visual presentation and layout of HTML elements within a web page. This section provides an introduction to CSS and its key concepts.

CSS is a style sheet language that defines how HTML elements should be displayed on the screen, in print, or in other media. It allows web developers to separate the structure and content of a web page (defined by HTML) from its visual presentation (defined by CSS). This separation of concerns makes it easier to maintain and update web pages.

Why Use CSS?

CSS offers several advantages:

1. **Consistency**: CSS enables consistent styling across multiple web pages by defining styles in a central location (an external stylesheet) and applying them to various HTML documents. This consistency enhances the user experience.

2. **Separation of Concerns**: By separating content (HTML) from presentation (CSS), web developers can focus on each aspect independently. This separation simplifies code maintenance and promotes a more organized development process.

3. **Responsive Design**: CSS allows developers to create responsive designs that adapt to different screen sizes and devices. This is essential for modern web applications that need to be accessible on a variety of devices, from desktop computers to mobile phones.

How CSS Works

CSS operates on the principle of selectors and declarations. Here's a basic overview:

- **Selectors**: Selectors are patterns used to select HTML elements to which a style should be applied. Selectors can target specific elements, classes of elements, or even all elements on a page.

- **Declarations**: Declarations consist of property-value pairs that define the style to be applied. For example, a declaration might specify that the font size should be 16 pixels or that the background color should be blue.

CSS rules consist of one or more selectors and a set of declarations enclosed in curly braces. Here's an example:

```
h1 {
    color: blue;
    font-size: 24px;
}
```

In this rule, the h1 selector targets all `<h1>` elements in the HTML document and applies the specified styles (blue text color and a font size of 24 pixels) to them.

CSS can be included in HTML documents in various ways:

1. **Inline CSS**: Styles can be applied directly to HTML elements using the `style` attribute. For example:

```
<p style="color: green;">This is a green paragraph.</p>
```

2. **Internal CSS**: CSS can be placed within a `<style>` element in the `<head>` section of an HTML document. This allows you to define styles that apply to that specific page. For example:

```
<head>
    <style>
        p {
            font-weight: bold;
        }
    </style>
</head>
<body>
    <p>This is a bold paragraph.</p>
</body>
```

3. **External CSS**: CSS can also be stored in separate external files with a `.css` extension. These external stylesheets can be linked to multiple HTML pages, promoting consistency in styling. For example:

```
<head>
    <link rel="stylesheet" type="text/css" href="styles.css">
</head>
```

In summary, CSS is a powerful tool for controlling the presentation of web pages. By understanding selectors, declarations, and the different ways to include CSS in web documents, you can effectively style your HTML content to create visually appealing and user-friendly websites.

Section 11.2: CSS Syntax and Declarations

To effectively use CSS for styling web pages, it's crucial to understand the syntax and structure of CSS rules and declarations. In this section, we'll delve into the details of CSS syntax and explore how to write CSS declarations.

A CSS rule consists of two main parts: a selector and a declaration block.

- **Selector**: The selector specifies which HTML elements the rule applies to. It defines the target of the styling. Selectors can be HTML element names (e.g., h1, p), class names (e.g., `.my-class`), IDs (e.g., `#my-id`), or other complex selectors.

- **Declaration Block**: The declaration block is enclosed in curly braces {} and contains one or more declarations. Each declaration consists of a property and a value, separated by a colon. Declarations are terminated with a semicolon ;. For example:

```
selector {
    property1: value1;
    property2: value2;
}
```

CSS Properties and Values

CSS offers a wide range of properties to control various aspects of element styling. Here are some common CSS properties:

- **color**: Specifies the text color, e.g., `color: blue;`.

- **font-size**: Sets the font size, e.g., `font-size: 16px;`.

- **font-family**: Defines the font family, e.g., `font-family: Arial, sans-serif;`.

- **background-color**: Sets the background color, e.g., `background-color: #f0f0f0;`.

- **margin**: Controls the space outside an element, e.g., `margin: 10px;`.

- **padding**: Specifies the space inside an element, e.g., `padding: 5px 10px;`.

- **border**: Defines the border around an element, e.g., `border: 1px solid #000;`.

CSS property values can be in various formats, including keywords, numeric values, colors, and more. For example:

- Keyword values: `font-style: italic;`

- Numeric values with units: `width: 300px;`

- Color values: `border-color: #ccc;`

- URLs for images: `background-image: url('image.jpg');`

CSS Comments

Comments in CSS allow you to add explanatory notes within your stylesheets. CSS comments are not displayed in the browser and are for developer documentation only. They can be helpful for explaining complex styles or leaving reminders.

CSS comments come in two formats:

1. Single-line comments, which start with //:

```
/* This is a single-line comment */
```

2. Multi-line comments, enclosed in /* */:

```
/*
This is a
multi-line comment
*/
```

Grouping Selectors

CSS allows you to group multiple selectors together in a single rule. This can be useful to apply the same styles to multiple elements. To group selectors, separate them with commas. For example:

```css
h1, h2, h3 {
    font-family: 'Roboto', sans-serif;
    font-weight: bold;
}
```

In this example, the styles for h1, h2, and h3 elements are defined in a single rule.

Specificity and Cascading

Understanding the concept of specificity is essential in CSS. Specificity determines which CSS rule should be applied when multiple conflicting rules target the same element. Specificity is calculated based on the combination of selectors and their order of appearance.

In cases of conflicting rules, the rule with the highest specificity wins. Specificity is often represented as a four-part value, with higher values taking precedence.

In addition to specificity, the "cascading" part of CSS refers to how styles are applied in a cascading manner. Styles can be inherited from parent elements or overridden by more specific rules.

In summary, mastering CSS syntax and understanding how to write CSS declarations, including properties, values, comments, and selectors, is essential for effective web page styling. Additionally, grasping specificity and the cascading nature of CSS will help you control how styles are applied when working with complex stylesheets.

Section 11.3: CSS Selectors and Specificity

CSS selectors play a fundamental role in specifying which HTML elements on a web page should receive styling. In this section, we'll explore CSS selectors in-depth and discuss the concept of specificity, which determines the order of precedence when conflicting styles are applied.

Simple Selectors

1. **Element Selector**: *The simplest selector targets HTML elements by their tag name. For example, to select all <p> elements:*
```
p {
    /* CSS rules here */
}
```

2. **Class Selector**: *Class selectors target elements with a specific class attribute. They are prefixed with a dot . followed by the class name. For example, to select all elements with the class "highlight":*
```
.highlight {
    /* CSS rules here */
}
```

3. **ID Selector**: *ID selectors target a single element with a unique ID attribute. They are prefixed with a hash # followed by the ID name. For example, to select an element with the ID "header":*
```
#header {
    /* CSS rules here */
}
```

4. **Universal Selector**: *The universal selector * selects all elements on the page. Use it sparingly, as it can lead to performance issues if overused.*
```
* {
    /* CSS rules here */
}
```

Combinators

Combinators allow you to target elements based on their relationship to other elements. There are four main types of combinators:

5. **Descendant Combinator (Whitespace)**: *Selects an element that is a descendant of another element.*
```
.container p {
    /* CSS rules here */
}
```

6. **Child Combinator (>)**: *Selects an element that is a direct child of another element.*
```
.menu > ul {
    /* CSS rules here */
}
```

7. Adjacent Sibling Combinator (+): *Selects an element that is an immediate sibling of another element.*

```
h2 + p {
    /* CSS rules here */
}
```

8. General Sibling Combinator (~): *Selects elements that are siblings of another element.*

```
h2 ~ p {
    /* CSS rules here */
}
```

Pseudo-classes and Pseudo-elements

9. Pseudo-classes: *Pseudo-classes allow you to target elements based on their state or position. For example, :hover selects an element when the mouse pointer is over it.*

```
a:hover {
    /* CSS rules here */
}
```

10. Pseudo-elements: *Pseudo-elements target specific parts of an element, such as the first line or first letter. They are denoted with double colons ::.*

```
p::first-line {
    /* CSS rules here */
}
```

Specificity

Specificity is a measure of the importance of a CSS rule, and it determines which styles are applied when conflicting rules exist. Specificity is calculated based on the following factors:

- **Inline Styles**: Styles applied directly to an element using the `style` attribute have the highest specificity.

- **ID Selectors**: ID selectors have a higher specificity than class selectors and element selectors.

- **Class Selectors and Attribute Selectors**: Class selectors and attribute selectors have the same specificity.

- **Element Selectors and Pseudo-elements/Pseudo-classes**: Element selectors have the lowest specificity. Pseudo-elements and pseudo-classes have a specificity between element selectors and class/attribute selectors.

- **Combined Selectors**: Specificity is cumulative when selectors are combined. For example, `div.container` has a higher specificity than just `.container`.

When conflicting styles are encountered, the rule with the highest specificity takes precedence. If specificity is the same, the rule that appears later in the stylesheet wins (cascading order).

Understanding CSS selectors and specificity is essential for creating maintainable and predictable stylesheets. By using the appropriate selectors and managing specificity effectively, you can avoid styling conflicts and ensure that your web pages are styled as intended.

Section 11.4: Styling Text and Backgrounds

In this section, we'll delve into the world of text and background styling using CSS. CSS provides a wide range of properties to control the appearance of text, including fonts, colors, text alignment, and spacing. Additionally, we'll explore techniques for customizing background styles to enhance the visual appeal of your web pages.

Styling Text

1. *Font Properties*: CSS allows you to specify the font family, font size, font weight, and font style for text elements. Here's an example of how to set the font properties for a paragraph:

```css
p {
    font-family: "Arial", sans-serif;
    font-size: 16px;
    font-weight: bold;
    font-style: italic;
}
```

- `font-family` defines the preferred font and fallback fonts.
- `font-size` sets the size of the text.
- `font-weight` adjusts the thickness of the text (e.g., `bold` or `normal`).
- `font-style` can make the text italic.

2. *Text Color*: You can change the color of text using the `color` property:

```css
p {
    color: #FF5733; /* Hexadecimal color code */
}
```

3. *Text Alignment*: Control the alignment of text within an element using the `text-align` property:

```css
h1 {
    text-align: center;
}
```

Common values for `text-align` include `left`, `right`, `center`, and `justify`.

4. *Text Decoration*: You can add text decoration, such as underlines or overlines, using the `text-decoration` property:

```css
a {
    text-decoration: underline;
}
```

Other values for text-decoration include overline, line-through, and none.

Styling Backgrounds

5. *Background Color: Change the background color of an element with the background-color property:*
```
.highlight {
    background-color: #FFFF00; /* Yellow background */
}
```

6. *Background Image: You can set a background image for an element using the background-image property:*
```
.header {
    background-image: url("header-bg.jpg");
}
```

You can control properties like background-repeat, background-size, and background-position to customize how the image is displayed.

7. *Background Gradient: CSS allows you to create gradient backgrounds using the linear-gradient() or radial-gradient() functions:*
```
.gradient-bg {
    background: linear-gradient(to bottom, #FF5733, #FFFF00);
}
```

This example creates a vertical linear gradient from red to yellow.

8. *Background Shorthand: You can use the background shorthand property to set multiple background-related properties in one declaration:*
```
.section {
    background: #FFFFFF url("section-bg.jpg") no-repeat center/cover;
}
```

In this example, we set the background color, image, no repetition, center alignment, and cover sizing all at once.

Styling text and backgrounds is essential for creating visually appealing and readable web pages. CSS offers extensive capabilities to tailor the appearance of text and backgrounds to match your design requirements. By mastering these CSS properties, you can craft engaging and user-friendly websites.

Section 11.5: Applying CSS to Multiple Elements

In this section, we'll explore techniques for applying CSS styles to multiple HTML elements efficiently. CSS allows you to target specific elements or groups of elements using selectors. These selectors can be based on element type, class, or ID. We'll also delve into pseudo-classes and pseudo-elements, which add dynamic styles and fine-grained control to your CSS.

Universal Selector

The universal selector (*) is a wildcard that matches all HTML elements on a page. While it's powerful, it should be used sparingly, as it can affect every element and impact performance. Here's an example:

```css
* {
    margin: 0;
    padding: 0;
    box-sizing: border-box;
}
```

In this example, we set all elements to have zero margins, zero padding, and use the border-box box model.

Type Selectors

Type selectors target all elements of a specific type. For instance, you can style all p (paragraph) elements like this:

```css
p {
    font-family: Arial, sans-serif;
}
```

Class Selectors

Class selectors allow you to target elements with a specific class attribute. This is useful for styling multiple elements that share a common class:

```css
.button {
    background-color: #0077FF;
    color: white;
    padding: 10px 20px;
}
```

In this case, all elements with class="button" will inherit these styles.

ID Selectors

ID selectors target a single unique element with a specific id attribute:

```css
#header {
    background-color: #333;
    color: white;
    padding: 20px;
}
```

Using IDs should be reserved for unique elements because, by definition, IDs should only be applied to one element per page.

Grouping Selectors

You can group selectors to apply the same styles to multiple elements. Separate them with commas:

```
h2, h3, h4 {
    font-weight: bold;
}
```

In this example, font-weight: bold is applied to all h2, h3, and h4 elements.

Pseudo-classes and Pseudo-elements

Pseudo-classes and pseudo-elements provide dynamic and fine-grained styling. Examples include :hover, :active, :first-child, ::before, and ::after. Here's how to style a link on hover:

```
a:hover {
    text-decoration: underline;
}
```

Descendant and Child Selectors

You can target nested elements using descendant () and child (>) selectors. For example, to style all p elements inside a div with the class container:

```
.container p {
    margin-bottom: 10px;
}
```

This will affect only p elements that are descendants of elements with the class container.

By understanding and effectively using CSS selectors, you can apply styles precisely and efficiently across your web pages, ensuring a consistent and visually appealing design.

Chapter 12: CSS Layout and Positioning

Section 12.1: Box Model in CSS

In web development, the Box Model is a fundamental concept that defines how elements on a web page are structured and how they interact with each other. Understanding the Box Model is essential for creating layouts and positioning elements with CSS.

Box Model Basics

The Box Model describes each HTML element as a rectangular box that consists of four main parts:

1. **Content**: This is the innermost part of the box and contains the actual content, such as text, images, or other HTML elements.

2. **Padding**: Padding is the space between the content and the element's border. You can set padding on all sides (top, right, bottom, left) independently.

3. **Border**: The border surrounds the padding and content. It can be styled with various properties like color, width, and style.

4. **Margin**: Margin is the space outside the border, creating a gap between the element and other nearby elements. Like padding, you can set margin on all sides.

Box Model Properties

To control the Box Model, CSS provides several properties:

- `width` and `height`: These properties determine the width and height of the content box.
- `padding`: Sets the padding around the content box.
- `border`: Configures the border of the box.
- `margin`: Defines the margin outside the border.
- `box-sizing`: Determines how the `width` and `height` properties apply. The default is `content-box`, where `width` and `height` only affect the content box. Setting it to `border-box` includes padding and border in the dimensions.

Example:

Let's create a simple example to illustrate the Box Model:

```
<!DOCTYPE html>
<html>
<head>
    <style>
        .box {
            width: 200px;
```

```
        height: 100px;
        padding: 20px;
        border: 2px solid #333;
        margin: 10px;
        box-sizing: border-box;
      }
    </style>
  </head>
  <body>
    <div class="box">
        This is a box with content.
    </div>
  </body>
</html>
```

In this example, we have a `<div>` element with a class of box. We apply `width`, `height`, padding, border, margin, and `box-sizing` properties to create a box with specific dimensions and spacing.

Understanding and effectively using the Box Model is crucial for building well-structured and visually appealing web layouts. It allows you to control the spacing and positioning of elements precisely.

Section 12.2: CSS Display Properties

In CSS, the `display` property is used to control how an element is rendered in the web page's layout. Understanding the different values of the `display` property is essential for creating flexible and responsive layouts.

Block-level and Inline-level Elements

CSS elements are categorized into two main types: block-level and inline-level.

- **Block-level Elements**: Block-level elements create a new "block" formatting context and typically start on a new line, extending the full width of their parent container. Common block-level elements include `<div>`, `<p>`, `<h1>` to `<h6>`, and `<ul>`.

- **Inline-level Elements**: Inline-level elements, on the other hand, do not start on a new line and only take up as much width as necessary. Examples of inline-level elements include `<span>`, `<a>`, `<strong>`, and `<em>`.

Common display Property Values

1. `display: block;`: This value makes an element a block-level element, causing it to start on a new line and extend the full width of its parent container.

2. `display: inline;`: This value makes an element an inline-level element, allowing it to flow within the content of a line and only take up as much width as necessary.

3. **display: inline-block;**: This value combines aspects of both block and inline elements. It behaves like an inline element but can have block-level properties like width and height.

4. **display: none;**: This value completely hides the element from the layout, making it invisible and not taking up any space. It's often used for hiding elements dynamically with JavaScript.

5. **display: flex;**: This value establishes a flex container, allowing you to create flexible and responsive layouts using the Flexbox model.

6. **display: grid;**: This value establishes a grid container, enabling you to create grid-based layouts using the CSS Grid layout system.

Example:

Let's see an example that demonstrates the use of the display property:

```html
<!DOCTYPE html>
<html>
<head>
    <style>
        .block {
            display: block;
            width: 200px;
            background-color: #f2f2f2;
            padding: 10px;
            margin-bottom: 10px;
        }

        .inline {
            display: inline;
            background-color: #ccc;
            padding: 5px;
        }
    </style>
</head>
<body>
    <div class="block">
        This is a block-level element.
    </div>
    <span class="inline">
        This is an inline-level element.
    </span>
</body>
</html>
```

In this example, we have a block-level <div> and an inline-level <span> element. The display property is applied to both, affecting how they are displayed in the layout. Block-level elements start on new lines, while inline-level elements stay within the text flow.

Section 12.3: Positioning Elements

In web development, positioning elements is a crucial part of creating the layout for your web pages. CSS provides several properties to control the position of elements, allowing you to precisely place them where you want within the document flow.

The position Property

The position property is used to specify the positioning method for an element. It can take several values:

1. **position: static;**: This is the default value. Elements with position: static; are positioned according to the normal flow of the document. They ignore the top, right, bottom, and left properties.

2. **position: relative;**: Elements with position: relative; are positioned relative to their normal position in the document flow. You can use the top, right, bottom, and left properties to offset them from their original position.

3. **position: absolute;**: Elements with position: absolute; are removed from the normal document flow and positioned relative to the nearest ancestor with a non-static position. If no such ancestor exists, it's positioned relative to the initial containing block (usually the viewport).

4. **position: fixed;**: Elements with position: fixed; are similar to position: absolute;, but they are always positioned relative to the viewport. This means they stay in the same position even when the page is scrolled.

5. **position: sticky;**: Elements with position: sticky; are positioned based on the user's scroll position. They behave like position: relative; until they reach a specified threshold (e.g., top of the viewport), at which point they become position: fixed;.

Example:

Here's an example that demonstrates the use of the position property:

```
<!DOCTYPE html>
<html>
<head>
    <style>
        .container {
            width: 300px;
            height: 200px;
            background-color: #f2f2f2;
            position: relative;
        }
```

```css
.box {
    width: 50px;
    height: 50px;
    background-color: #3498db;
}

.relative-box {
    position: relative;
    top: 30px;
    left: 30px;
}

.absolute-box {
    position: absolute;
    top: 20px;
    left: 20px;
}

.fixed-box {
    position: fixed;
    top: 10px;
    right: 10px;
}

.sticky-box {
    position: sticky;
    top: 100px;
}
    </style>
</head>
<body>
    <div class="container">
        <div class="box relative-box"></div>
        <div class="box absolute-box"></div>
        <div class="box fixed-box"></div>
        <div class="box sticky-box"></div>
    </div>
</body>
</html>
```

In this example, we have a container with four boxes, each using a different position value. The .relative-box is positioned relative to its normal position, the .absolute-box is positioned absolutely within its container, the .fixed-box is fixed to the viewport, and the .sticky-box becomes fixed when scrolling past its position. These properties allow for versatile layout design.

Section 12.4: Floats and Clearing

Floats are CSS properties that were originally intended for text wrapping around images, but they have since been used for creating various layout designs. Floats allow elements to be shifted to the left or right, which can be helpful in creating multi-column layouts or positioning elements next to each other.

The float Property

The float property is used to specify whether an element should be floated to the left, right, or not at all. It can take the following values:

- **float: left;**: This floats the element to the left, allowing content to flow around it on the right side. It's often used for creating multi-column layouts.

- **float: right;**: This floats the element to the right, allowing content to flow around it on the left side.

- **float: none;**: This is the default value and means that the element should not float. It stays in the normal flow of the document.

Clearing Floats

One common issue when using floats is the need to "clear" them. When an element is floated, it can cause its parent container to collapse if it doesn't have a defined height. To fix this, you often need to clear the floats.

You can use the clear property to specify whether an element should be placed below any floated elements that precede it in the document flow. It can take the following values:

- **clear: left;**: This clears any left-floated elements that precede the element, forcing it to appear below them.

- **clear: right;**: This clears any right-floated elements that precede the element, forcing it to appear below them.

- **clear: both;**: This clears both left and right-floated elements that precede the element, ensuring it appears below them.

Example:

Here's an example that demonstrates the use of floats and clearing:

```
<!DOCTYPE html>
<html>
<head>
    <style>
        .container {
            width: 400px;
```

```css
            background-color: #f2f2f2;
            overflow: hidden; /* Clear floats */
        }

        .box {
            width: 150px;
            height: 150px;
            margin: 10px;
            background-color: #3498db;
            float: left;
        }

        .clear-box {
            clear: both; /* Clear floats */
        }
    </style>
</head>
<body>
    <div class="container">
        <div class="box"></div>
        <div class="box"></div>
        <div class="box"></div>
        <div class="clear-box"></div>
    </div>
</body>
</html>
```

In this example, we have a container with three floated boxes. To prevent the container from collapsing due to the floated elements, we use the overflow: hidden; property. Additionally, we've added a .clear-box element with clear: both; to ensure it appears below the floated boxes. This is a common technique for creating layouts with floats.

Section 12.5: Creating Responsive Layouts

Responsive web design is an essential aspect of modern web development. It ensures that your website looks and functions well on various devices, from desktop computers to smartphones and tablets. In this section, we'll explore techniques for creating responsive layouts using CSS.

Media Queries

Media queries are a fundamental part of responsive design. They allow you to apply different styles to your web page based on the characteristics of the user's device, such as its screen width. Media queries use the @media rule in CSS and follow the syntax:

```css
@media screen and (max-width: 600px) {
    /* CSS rules for screens with a maximum width of 600px */
}
```

In the example above, the CSS rules inside the media query will only apply if the screen's width is 600 pixels or less. You can also use `min-width` and combine multiple conditions to create complex responsive layouts.

Fluid Grids

One of the key principles of responsive design is creating fluid grids. Instead of specifying fixed pixel widths for elements, you use percentages or other relative units like `em` or `rem`. For example, to create a two-column layout, you might use:

```css
.column {
    width: 50%;
    float: left;
}
```

This ensures that each column takes up 50% of the container's width, making it adapt to different screen sizes.

Flexbox and CSS Grid

Flexbox and CSS Grid are powerful tools for creating responsive layouts. Flexbox is particularly useful for handling the alignment and distribution of items within a container, while CSS Grid provides a two-dimensional grid system for creating complex layouts.

```css
.container {
    display: flex;
    flex-wrap: wrap;
}

.column {
    flex: 1;
    /* Additional styles for columns */
}
```

In this example, we use Flexbox to create a responsive grid layout where columns automatically adjust their width based on the available space.

Mobile-First Design

A best practice in responsive design is to follow a mobile-first approach. Start by designing and coding for mobile devices with small screens and then progressively enhance the layout for larger screens using media queries. This ensures that your website is optimized for mobile users and gracefully adapts to larger screens.

Testing and Debugging

Testing your responsive layouts on various devices and browsers is crucial. There are many browser developer tools and online testing services available to help you preview and debug your responsive designs. Additionally, pay attention to performance considerations for responsive images and content delivery.

Responsive web design is an ongoing process, and it's essential to keep user experience in mind as you adapt your layouts to different devices. By following these principles and techniques, you can create web experiences that are accessible and visually appealing across a wide range of screens.

Chapter 13: CSS Flexbox and Grid

In this chapter, we'll dive into two powerful CSS layout technologies: Flexbox and Grid. These layout systems have revolutionized how we design and structure web page layouts. They provide flexible and responsive options for creating complex layouts with ease.

Section 13.1: Understanding Flexbox

Flexbox, short for **Flexible Box Layout**, is a one-dimensional layout model. It allows you to design complex layouts with a more efficient and predictable way than traditional CSS approaches. With Flexbox, you work with a parent container and its child elements, which become **flex items**.

The Flex Container

To create a flex layout, you first need a **flex container**. You can turn any HTML element into a flex container by applying the `display: flex;` or `display: inline-flex;` property to it. For example:

```
.container {
    display: flex;
}
```

Now, all direct children of the `.container` element will become flex items, and the container itself becomes a **flex container**. The flex items can be aligned and distributed within this container along a single axis (either horizontally or vertically).

The Main Axis and Cross Axis

In a flex container, you have two main axes: the **main axis** and the **cross axis**. The main axis is defined by the `flex-direction` property, which can be set to row (default), row-reverse, column, or column-reverse. The cross axis is perpendicular to the main axis.

Flex Items

Flex items within a flex container can have different sizes and can be rearranged to fit the available space. You control how they behave on the main axis using properties like `flex-grow`, `flex-shrink`, and `flex-basis`.

Here's a simple example of creating a flex container with three flex items:

```
<div class="container">
    <div class="item">Item 1</div>
    <div class="item">Item 2</div>
    <div class="item">Item 3</div>
</div>

.container {
    display: flex;
```

```
    justify-content: space-between; /* Distribute items along the main axis *
/
    align-items: center; /* Center items along the cross axis */
}

.item {
    flex: 1; /* Each item takes up an equal amount of available space */
}
```

In this example, the `justify-content` property distributes the flex items along the main axis with equal space between them, and the `align-items` property centers them along the cross axis.

Flexbox is incredibly versatile and can be used for a wide range of layout scenarios, including navigation menus, card layouts, and even entire page structures. In the next sections, we'll explore more advanced aspects of Flexbox and also introduce CSS Grid for two-dimensional layouts.

Section 13.2: Flexbox Properties

In the previous section, we introduced the basics of Flexbox and how to create a flex container and flex items. Now, let's dive deeper into the various properties that allow you to control the layout and behavior of flex items within a flex container.

1. flex-direction

The `flex-direction` property defines the main axis along which flex items are placed. It can take one of four values: - `row` (default): Items are placed along the horizontal main axis. - `row-reverse`: Items are placed along the horizontal main axis in reverse order. - `column`: Items are placed along the vertical main axis. - `column-reverse`: Items are placed along the vertical main axis in reverse order.

Example:

```
.container {
    display: flex;
    flex-direction: row-reverse;
}
```

2. justify-content

The `justify-content` property controls how flex items are distributed along the main axis. It has several possible values: - `flex-start` (default): Items are packed toward the start of the main axis. - `flex-end`: Items are packed toward the end of the main axis. - `center`: Items are centered along the main axis. - `space-between`: Items are evenly distributed with the first item at the start and the last item at the end. - `space-around`: Items are evenly distributed with equal space around them.

Example:

```
.container {
    display: flex;
    justify-content: center;
}
```

3. align-items

The align-items property controls how flex items are aligned along the cross axis. It has several possible values: - stretch (default): Items are stretched to fill the cross-axis. - flex-start: Items are aligned at the start of the cross axis. - flex-end: Items are aligned at the end of the cross axis. - center: Items are centered along the cross axis. - baseline: Items are aligned such that their baselines align.

Example:

```
.container {
    display: flex;
    align-items: center;
}
```

4. flex

The flex property is a shorthand property for setting flex-grow, flex-shrink, and flex-basis in one declaration. It defines how a flex item should grow or shrink relative to other items.

Example:

```
.item {
    flex: 1 1 0;
}
```

5. flex-grow and flex-shrink

The flex-grow property determines how much a flex item should grow relative to other items when there's extra space along the main axis. The flex-shrink property determines how much a flex item should shrink relative to other items when there's not enough space along the main axis.

Example:

```
.item {
    flex-grow: 2; /* This item will grow twice as much as other items */
    flex-shrink: 0; /* This item won't shrink */
}
```

These are just a few of the many properties available for controlling Flexbox layouts. Flexbox is a flexible and powerful layout model that can be customized to suit a wide range of design requirements. In the next section, we'll explore CSS Grid, another layout technology that's especially well-suited for two-dimensional layouts.

Section 13.3: Creating Flexbox Layouts

In the previous section, we covered essential Flexbox properties and how they can be used to control the layout of flex items within a flex container. Now, let's explore how to create practical layouts using Flexbox.

1. Simple Horizontal and Vertical Centering

One of the most common use cases for Flexbox is centering content both horizontally and vertically within a container. To achieve this, you can set display: flex on the container and use the properties justify-content: center for horizontal centering and align-items: center for vertical centering.

```css
.container {
    display: flex;
    justify-content: center; /* Horizontal centering */
    align-items: center; /* Vertical centering */
}
```

2. Creating Equal-Width Columns

Flexbox makes it easy to create equal-width columns within a container. You can set flex: 1 on the child elements to distribute available space equally among them.

```css
.column {
    flex: 1; /* Equal width columns */
}
```

3. Building a Navigation Bar

Flexbox is handy for creating responsive navigation bars. You can use it to distribute navigation items evenly across the horizontal space, ensuring they adapt to different screen sizes.

```html
<div class="navbar">
    <a href="#">Home</a>
    <a href="#">About</a>
    <a href="#">Services</a>
    <a href="#">Contact</a>
</div>
```

```css
.navbar {
    display: flex;
    justify-content: space-around; /* Evenly spaced navigation items */
}
```

4. Implementing a Sticky Footer

Creating a sticky footer that remains at the bottom of the page, regardless of content height, is a common layout requirement. Flexbox simplifies this task.

```css
html, body {
    height: 100%;
    margin: 0;
}

.page-content {
    flex: 1; /* Expand to fill available space */
}

.footer {
    flex-shrink: 0; /* Don't allow the footer to shrink */
}
```

5. Responsive Card Layout

Flexbox can be used to create responsive card layouts where the number of columns adjusts based on screen width.

```css
.card-container {
    display: flex;
    flex-wrap: wrap; /* Wrap to the next row when no more space */
}

.card {
    flex: 1; /* Equal-width cards */
    margin: 10px; /* Add some spacing between cards */
}
```

These are just a few examples of how Flexbox can simplify complex layout tasks in web development. By combining various Flexbox properties creatively, you can achieve a wide range of responsive and dynamic layouts for your web projects. In the next section, we'll explore another powerful layout technology: CSS Grid.

Section 13.4: Introduction to CSS Grid

CSS Grid is a powerful layout system that allows you to create two-dimensional grid-based layouts with ease. It's well-suited for creating complex designs, such as magazine-style layouts or any layout that requires precise control over both rows and columns.

1. Grid Container and Grid Items

In CSS Grid, the container element becomes a grid container by setting `display: grid`. This container holds grid items that can be placed anywhere within the grid. By default, grid items flow in a row-based layout.

```css
.grid-container {
    display: grid; /* Create a grid container */
}
```

2. Defining Grid Rows and Columns

To define the structure of the grid, you can specify the size of rows and columns using properties like `grid-template-rows` and `grid-template-columns`. You can use various units like pixels, percentages, or `fr` (fractional unit).

```css
.grid-container {
    display: grid;
    grid-template-rows: 1fr 2fr; /* Two rows with 1:2 height ratio */
    grid-template-columns: 1fr 2fr; /* Two columns with 1:2 width ratio */
}
```

3. Placing Grid Items

Grid items can be placed within the grid using the `grid-row` and `grid-column` properties, specifying their starting and ending positions.

```css
.grid-item {
    grid-row: 1 / 2; /* Starts at row 1 and ends at row 2 */
    grid-column: 2 / 3; /* Starts at column 2 and ends at column 3 */
}
```

4. Grid Gaps

You can add gaps (margins) between grid rows and columns using the `grid-row-gap` and `grid-column-gap` properties.

```css
.grid-container {
    display: grid;
    grid-row-gap: 10px; /* Gap between rows */
    grid-column-gap: 20px; /* Gap between columns */
}
```

5. Grid Areas

CSS Grid also allows you to define named grid areas and place items in those areas. This is particularly useful for creating complex layouts with clear semantics.

```css
.grid-container {
    display: grid;
    grid-template-areas:
        "header header"
```

```
        "sidebar main"
        "footer footer";
}

.header {
    grid-area: header; /* Places the item in the 'header' area */
}

.main {
    grid-area: main; /* Places the item in the 'main' area */
}

.footer {
    grid-area: footer; /* Places the item in the 'footer' area */
}
```

6. Responsive Grids

One of the strengths of CSS Grid is its responsiveness. You can easily change the grid structure based on screen size using media queries.

```
@media (max-width: 768px) {
    .grid-container {
        grid-template-areas:
            "header"
            "main"
            "footer";
    }
}
```

7. Browser Support

CSS Grid is widely supported in modern browsers, making it a valuable tool for creating versatile layouts. For older browsers, you can provide fallback styles or use feature detection to provide alternative layouts.

In the next section, we'll delve deeper into advanced CSS Grid techniques and explore how to create more complex grid-based layouts.

Section 13.5: Grid Layout Examples

In this section, we'll explore some practical examples of using CSS Grid layout to create various types of layouts. CSS Grid's flexibility allows you to create complex designs with relative ease. Let's dive into these examples:

1. Basic Grid Layout

```
<div class="grid-container">
    <div class="item">1</div>
```

```
    <div class="item">2</div>
    <div class="item">3</div>
    <div class="item">4</div>
    <div class="item">5</div>
    <div class="item">6</div>
</div>

.grid-container {
    display: grid;
    grid-template-columns: repeat(3, 1fr); /* 3 columns with equal width */
    grid-gap: 10px; /* Gap between grid items */
}

.item {
    background-color: #3498db;
    color: #fff;
    padding: 20px;
    text-align: center;
}
```

This creates a basic grid layout with three columns and two rows. The `repeat` function simplifies the definition of multiple equal-width columns.

2. Responsive Grid Layout

```
<div class="grid-container">
    <div class="item">1</div>
    <div class="item">2</div>
    <div class="item">3</div>
    <div class="item">4</div>
</div>

.grid-container {
    display: grid;
    grid-template-columns: repeat(auto-fit, minmax(200px, 1fr)); /* Responsiv
e columns */
    grid-gap: 10px; /* Gap between grid items */
}

.item {
    background-color: #e74c3c;
    color: #fff;
    padding: 20px;
    text-align: center;
}
```

In this example, the `auto-fit` and `minmax` functions create a responsive grid that adjusts the number of columns based on available space.

3. Complex Grid Layout

```html
<div class="grid-container">
    <div class="header">Header</div>
    <div class="sidebar">Sidebar</div>
    <div class="main">Main Content</div>
    <div class="footer">Footer</div>
</div>
```

```css
.grid-container {
    display: grid;
    grid-template-columns: 1fr 3fr; /* Two columns with different widths */
    grid-template-rows: auto 1fr auto; /* Three rows with different heights */
    grid-template-areas:
        "header header"
        "sidebar main"
        "footer footer";
    grid-gap: 20px; /* Gap between grid items */
}

.header {
    grid-area: header;
    background-color: #2ecc71;
    color: #fff;
    padding: 20px;
}

.sidebar {
    grid-area: sidebar;
    background-color: #f1c40f;
    padding: 20px;
}

.main {
    grid-area: main;
    background-color: #3498db;
    color: #fff;
    padding: 20px;
}

.footer {
    grid-area: footer;
    background-color: #34495e;
    color: #fff;
    padding: 20px;
}
```

This example demonstrates a more complex layout with header, sidebar, main content, and footer sections, each with distinct styling.

4. Grid for Photo Gallery

```html
<div class="grid-container">
    <div class="item">1</div>
    <div class="item">2</div>
    <div class="item">3</div>
    <!-- Add more items for your gallery -->
</div>
```

```css
.grid-container {
    display: grid;
    grid-template-columns: repeat(auto-fill, minmax(200px, 1fr)); /* Responsi
ve grid */
    grid-gap: 10px; /* Gap between grid items */
}

.item {
    background-color: #f39c12;
    padding: 10px;
    text-align: center;
    color: #fff;
}
```

This example creates a responsive photo gallery grid where images or items can be added dynamically.

These examples showcase the versatility of CSS Grid in creating different layouts for various web design needs. By combining grid properties and techniques, you can achieve intricate designs with ease. Experiment and adapt these concepts to your specific projects for optimal results.

Chapter 14: CSS Transitions and Animations

Section 14.1: Transitioning CSS Properties

CSS Transitions and animations allow you to add dynamic and engaging visual effects to your web pages. In this section, we'll explore CSS transitions, which enable smooth property changes over a specified duration. Transitions are often used for hover effects, menu animations, and more.

Understanding CSS Transitions

A CSS transition gradually changes the property values of an element from one state to another. It provides a smoother transition between these states, making the change visually pleasing.

To create a basic transition, you specify the CSS properties to transition, the duration of the transition, and the timing function that defines the transition's pace.

Here's the general syntax for defining a transition:

```css
/* Property to transition */
element {
    transition-property: property1, property2, ...;
    /* Duration in seconds (s) or milliseconds (ms) */
    transition-duration: duration;
    /* Timing function (easing) */
    transition-timing-function: timing-function;
}
```

- transition-property: Specifies the CSS properties to transition (e.g., color, width, opacity).
- transition-duration: Sets the duration of the transition effect (e.g., 0.5s, 200ms).
- transition-timing-function: Defines the pacing of the transition (e.g., ease, linear, ease-in-out).

Example: Hover Effect

Let's create a simple hover effect that changes the background color of a button when hovered over:

```html
<!DOCTYPE html>
<html>
<head>
    <style>
        /* Define the button styles */
        .button {
            background-color: #3498db;
            color: #fff;
```

```
            padding: 10px 20px;
            text-align: center;
            display: inline-block;
            transition: background-color 0.3s ease; /* Define the transition
*/
        }

        /* Apply the transition on hover */
        .button:hover {
            background-color: #e74c3c;
        }
    </style>
</head>
<body>
    <button class="button">Hover Me</button>
</body>
</html>
```

In this example, the button's background color smoothly transitions from #3498db to #e74c3c over a duration of 0.3s with an easing function of ease when hovered over.

Transitioning Multiple Properties

You can transition multiple properties simultaneously by specifying them in the transition-property property. For instance, you can transition both color and width:

```
element {
    transition-property: color, width;
    transition-duration: 0.5s;
    transition-timing-function: ease-in-out;
}
```

Customizing Transition Delays

CSS transitions also allow you to customize the delay before the transition starts using the transition-delay property. This can be useful for creating more complex animations.

```
element {
    transition-property: property1;
    transition-duration: 0.5s;
    transition-delay: 0.2s; /* Delay of 0.2 seconds before the transition sta
rts */
    transition-timing-function: ease-in-out;
}
```

CSS transitions are a valuable tool for adding subtle and interactive effects to your web pages. Experiment with different properties, durations, and timing functions to achieve the desired visual impact for your web elements.

Section 14.2: Keyframe Animations

Keyframe animations in CSS offer a powerful way to create intricate and dynamic animations for your web elements. Unlike transitions that only involve the start and end states of an element, keyframe animations allow you to define multiple intermediate states, or keyframes, resulting in complex and responsive animations.

Creating Keyframe Animations

To create a keyframe animation, you define a set of keyframes using the `@keyframes` rule. Each keyframe specifies the styles for an element at a certain point in time. You can name the animation for reference and assign it to elements using CSS properties.

Here's a basic example of a keyframe animation that moves an element across the screen:

```css
/* Define the animation */
@keyframes moveRight {
    0% {
        transform: translateX(0);
    }
    100% {
        transform: translateX(100px);
    }
}

/* Apply the animation to an element */
.element {
    animation: moveRight 2s linear infinite;
}
```

In this example: - `@keyframes moveRight` defines the animation and its keyframes. - `0%` and `100%` represent the starting and ending points of the animation. - `transform: translateX(0)` sets the initial position, and `transform: translateX(100px)` defines the final position. - `.element` applies the animation to an HTML element.

Animation Properties

You can control various aspects of keyframe animations using animation-related CSS properties:

- `animation-name`: Specifies the name of the animation defined with `@keyframes`.
- `animation-duration`: Sets the duration of the animation in seconds (s) or milliseconds (ms).
- `animation-timing-function`: Defines the pacing of the animation (e.g., `ease`, `linear`, `ease-in-out`).
- `animation-iteration-count`: Specifies how many times the animation should repeat (e.g., `infinite`, `3`).

- animation-direction: Determines whether the animation runs forwards, backwards, or alternates (e.g., normal, reverse, alternate).
- animation-delay: Adds a delay before the animation starts (e.g., 0.5s).

Example: Bouncing Ball Animation

Here's a more complex example of a bouncing ball animation:

```css
/* Define the bouncing animation */
@keyframes bounce {
    0%, 100% {
        transform: translateY(0);
    }
    50% {
        transform: translateY(-100px);
    }
}

/* Apply the animation to a ball element */
.ball {
    width: 50px;
    height: 50px;
    background-color: #3498db;
    border-radius: 50%;
    animation: bounce 2s ease-in-out infinite;
}
```

In this example, the ball element smoothly bounces up and down in an infinite loop.

Keyframe animations are versatile and can be used to create a wide range of animations, including fading, scaling, rotating, and more. Experiment with different keyframes and animation properties to bring your web pages to life with engaging and interactive animations.

Section 14.3: Creating Smooth Transitions

CSS transitions provide a simple and elegant way to add smooth animations to elements when their properties change. Transitions allow you to smoothly transition between different states, such as changing colors, sizes, or positions, creating a more visually appealing user experience.

Basics of CSS Transitions

To create a CSS transition, you need to specify the property you want to animate, the duration of the animation, and the timing function that controls the animation's pace. Here's a basic example:

```css
/* Define a transition on the background color property */
.element {
    background-color: #3498db;
    transition: background-color 0.3s ease;
}

/* Add a hover effect to change the background color */
.element:hover {
    background-color: #e74c3c;
}
```

In this example: - .element has a background color that transitions smoothly over 0.3 seconds with an ease timing function. - When you hover over .element, the background color changes smoothly to a new color.

Transition Properties

You can control various aspects of CSS transitions using the following properties:

- transition-property: Specifies which properties should be animated (e.g., color, width, opacity).
- transition-duration: Sets the duration of the transition in seconds (s) or milliseconds (ms).
- transition-timing-function: Defines the pacing of the transition (e.g., ease, linear, ease-in-out).
- transition-delay: Adds a delay before the transition starts (e.g., 0.2s).

Multiple Transitions

You can apply multiple transitions to the same element, animating different properties with their own durations and timing functions. For example:

```css
/* Define multiple transitions */
.element {
    width: 100px;
    height: 100px;
    background-color: #3498db;
    transition-property: width, height, background-color;
    transition-duration: 0.3s, 0.5s, 1s;
    transition-timing-function: ease, linear, ease-in-out;
}

/* Change properties on hover */
.element:hover {
    width: 200px;
    height: 200px;
    background-color: #e74c3c;
}
```

In this case, when hovering over `.element`, the width, height, and background color change with different durations and timing functions, resulting in a multi-dimensional animation.

Transitioning Multiple Properties

You can also transition multiple properties in a single shorthand property. For instance:

```
/* Define multiple transitions using shorthand */
.element {
    width: 100px;
    height: 100px;
    background-color: #3498db;
    transition: width 0.3s ease, height 0.5s linear, background-color 1s ease
-in-out;
}

/* Change properties on hover */
.element:hover {
    width: 200px;
    height: 200px;
    background-color: #e74c3c;
}
```

This approach keeps your CSS more concise and easier to read.

CSS transitions are a great way to enhance user interactions and provide visual feedback on web pages. They are particularly useful for creating smooth animations without the need for complex JavaScript code. Experiment with different transition properties and timing functions to achieve the desired visual effects in your web projects.

Section 14.4: Advanced Animation Techniques

While CSS transitions and keyframe animations cover the basics of animating elements on a webpage, advanced animation techniques allow you to create more complex and dynamic animations. In this section, we'll explore some advanced animation techniques using CSS and JavaScript.

1. CSS Animations with Keyframes

CSS keyframe animations provide fine-grained control over animations. They allow you to define multiple stages of an animation, specifying the style changes at different points in time. Here's a basic example:

```
/* Define a keyframe animation named 'move' */
@keyframes move {
    0% {
        transform: translateX(0);
    }
```

```
    50% {
        transform: translateX(100px);
    }
    100% {
        transform: translateX(0);
    }
}

/* Apply the 'move' animation to an element */
.element {
    animation: move 2s infinite;
}
```

In this example: - @keyframes move defines a keyframe animation called 'move' with three keyframes at 0%, 50%, and 100%. - .element applies the 'move' animation, causing it to move horizontally and loop infinitely.

2. Animation Properties

CSS animations offer several properties for controlling animations:

- animation-name: Specifies the name of the keyframe animation.
- animation-duration: Sets the duration of the animation.
- animation-timing-function: Defines the pacing of the animation.
- animation-delay: Adds a delay before the animation starts.
- animation-iteration-count: Sets the number of times the animation should repeat.
- animation-direction: Controls the direction of the animation (normal, reverse, alternate, alternate-reverse).
- animation-fill-mode: Determines the styles applied before and after the animation (none, forwards, backwards, both).

3. JavaScript Animation Libraries

For more complex and interactive animations, JavaScript animation libraries like GreenSock Animation Platform (GSAP) and Anime.js provide powerful tools. These libraries offer features like timeline control, easing functions, and physics-based animations.

Here's an example using GSAP:

```
<!-- Include GSAP Library -->
<script src="https://cdnjs.cloudflare.com/ajax/libs/gsap/3.9.1/gsap.min.js"></script>

<!-- HTML element to animate -->
<div class="element"></div>

<script>
```

```
// Create a GSAP timeline
const tl = gsap.timeline({ repeat: -1 });

// Define animation steps
tl.to(".element", { x: 100, duration: 1, ease: "power2.inOut" })
  .to(".element", { y: 100, duration: 1, ease: "elastic.out(1, 0.3)" })
  .to(".element", { x: 0, duration: 1, ease: "power2.inOut" })
  .to(".element", { y: 0, duration: 1, ease: "elastic.out(1, 0.3)" });
</script>
```

In this example, we create a GSAP timeline (tl) and define animation steps using the .to() method. The animation repeats indefinitely.

4. WebGL and 3D Animations

For highly immersive and 3D animations, WebGL and libraries like Three.js are popular choices. WebGL leverages hardware acceleration for smooth rendering of complex 3D scenes. Three.js simplifies working with WebGL, making it more accessible to web developers.

Advanced animations can add a layer of sophistication to your web projects, creating engaging user experiences. Consider the complexity and performance requirements of your animations when choosing between CSS, JavaScript libraries, or WebGL-based approaches.

Section 14.5: Browser Compatibility

Ensuring that your web animations work consistently across different browsers is essential for providing a seamless user experience. While modern browsers have made significant improvements in supporting animations, there are still some challenges to consider.

1. CSS Vendor Prefixes

One of the challenges in CSS animations is dealing with vendor prefixes. Different browsers may require different prefixes for CSS properties to work correctly. For example, you might need to use -webkit-, -moz-, or -ms- prefixes for certain properties.

```css
/* Example of CSS animation with vendor prefixes */
@keyframes move {
    0% {
        transform: translateX(0);
    }
    100% {
        transform: translateX(100px);
    }
}

.element {
    animation: move 2s infinite;
```

```
  -webkit-animation: move 2s infinite; /* Safari and older versions of Chro
me */
}
```

To address this, you can use tools like autoprefixer to automatically add the necessary
prefixes to your CSS during the build process.

2. Browser Testing Tools

Testing your animations on different browsers is crucial. Several browser testing tools and
services can help you identify and fix compatibility issues. Popular choices include
BrowserStack, CrossBrowserTesting, and Sauce Labs.

3. JavaScript Compatibility

When using JavaScript animations or libraries, be mindful of browser compatibility. Always
check the documentation of the library you're using to ensure it works as expected across
various browsers.

4. Graceful Degradation and Progressive Enhancement

To ensure a smooth user experience, consider using graceful degradation and progressive
enhancement techniques. This means that even if a user's browser doesn't support a
specific animation or feature, they can still access and use your website's core content and
functionality.

For example, if you have a complex JavaScript-based animation, provide an alternative
static representation for users with older browsers or those who have disabled JavaScript.
This ensures that your website remains functional for a broader audience.

5. Browser-Specific Bugs

Be aware of browser-specific bugs and limitations when implementing animations.
Browsers might interpret CSS or JavaScript differently, leading to unexpected behavior.
Refer to browser bug trackers or forums for workarounds and solutions if you encounter
such issues.

6. Progressive Enhancement with CSS Animations

For CSS animations, start with a simple, browser-compatible animation that enhances the
user experience. Then, use CSS feature queries (@supports) to check if the browser
supports more advanced animations. If it does, you can apply additional animations or
transitions.

```
/* Basic animation for all browsers */
.element {
    transition: transform 0.3s ease-in-out;
    transform: translateX(0);
}
```

```css
/* Additional animation for browsers that support it */
@supports (animation-name: move) {
    .element {
        animation: move 2s infinite;
    }
}
```

By following these best practices and testing thoroughly, you can create web animations that work smoothly across a wide range of browsers, ensuring a consistent and delightful user experience for your website visitors.

Chapter 15: Responsive Web Design

Section 15.1: What Is Responsive Web Design?

Responsive Web Design (RWD) is an approach to web design and development that focuses on creating web pages that look and function well on various devices and screen sizes. With the proliferation of smartphones, tablets, laptops, and desktop computers, it's crucial for websites to adapt to different screen dimensions and resolutions. RWD provides a solution to this challenge.

The Concept of Responsiveness

At the core of responsive web design is the concept of responsiveness. A responsive website is designed to respond to the user's device and screen size, providing an optimal viewing and interaction experience. Instead of creating separate websites or apps for different devices, RWD uses a single codebase to adapt to various contexts.

Key Principles of Responsive Design

1. **Fluid Grid Layouts**: In responsive design, the layout is based on a fluid grid system rather than fixed pixel values. This means that elements on the page are sized relative to their container, allowing them to adapt to different screen widths.

2. **Flexible Images and Media**: Images and multimedia content should also be flexible and scale with the screen size. CSS techniques like `max-width: 100%` are commonly used to achieve this.

3. **Media Queries**: Media queries are CSS rules that apply styles based on the characteristics of the device, such as screen width, height, and orientation. They enable designers to create breakpoints where the layout and design change to accommodate different screens.

4. **Mobile-First Approach**: Many responsive designs follow a mobile-first approach, where the initial design is optimized for small screens. As the screen size increases, additional layout and styling enhancements are applied.

Benefits of Responsive Web Design

Responsive web design offers several benefits:

- **Improved User Experience**: Users can access your website on any device without a degraded experience. This leads to higher user satisfaction and engagement.

- **Cost-Efficiency**: Maintaining a single codebase for all devices is more cost-effective than developing separate websites or apps.

- **SEO-Friendly**: Search engines like Google prioritize mobile-friendly websites in search results. Responsive design can improve your site's search engine rankings.

- **Easier Maintenance**: With one codebase to maintain, updates and changes are simpler and less time-consuming.

Responsive web design has become a standard practice in web development, ensuring that websites are accessible and functional for all users, regardless of the device they use. In the following sections, we'll delve deeper into the techniques and tools used in responsive design.

Section 15.2: Media Queries

Media queries are a fundamental part of responsive web design (RWD). They allow you to apply different styles and layouts to your web pages based on the characteristics of the user's device, such as screen size, resolution, and orientation. Media queries are written in CSS and are essential for creating a responsive and adaptable design.

Syntax of Media Queries

Media queries use the @media rule in CSS to specify conditions under which the enclosed styles should apply. Here's the basic syntax of a media query:

```
@media media-type and (media-feature) {
    /* CSS styles to apply when conditions are met */
}
```

- media-type: Specifies the type of media being targeted, such as screen, print, all, or others.

- media-feature: Defines the condition based on the characteristics of the user's device. Common media features include width, height, max-width, min-width, orientation, and more.

Using Media Features

Media features allow you to create breakpoints in your design, where different styles are applied as the screen size changes. For example, you can use the max-width media feature to apply styles to screens with a maximum width:

```
@media screen and (max-width: 768px) {
    /* Styles for screens with a width of 768px or less */
}
```

Combining Media Features

You can combine multiple media features to create more complex conditions. For instance, you might want to target screens with a minimum width of 768px and a landscape orientation:

```
@media screen and (min-width: 768px) and (orientation: landscape) {
    /* Styles for screens with a width of at least 768px in landscape orienta
tion */
}
```

Mobile-First Approach

A common practice in RWD is the "mobile-first" approach. This means designing for mobile devices first and then gradually enhancing the design for larger screens using media queries. This approach ensures that your website works well on small screens and progressively adapts to larger ones.

Examples of Media Queries

Here are some practical examples of media queries:

1. **Mobile Devices**:
```
@media screen and (max-width: 480px) {
    /* Styles for small mobile devices */
}
```

2. **Tablets**:
```
@media screen and (min-width: 481px) and (max-width: 1024px) {
    /* Styles for tablets */
}
```

3. **Desktops and Larger**:
```
@media screen and (min-width: 1025px) {
    /* Styles for desktop screens and larger */
}
```

Media queries are a powerful tool in responsive web design, allowing you to create flexible and adaptive layouts that provide an optimal user experience across various devices. By strategically using media queries, you can ensure that your website looks and functions well on screens of all sizes.

Section 15.3: Fluid Grid Layouts

Fluid grid layouts are a key aspect of responsive web design (RWD). They allow web designers and developers to create flexible and adaptable page layouts that automatically adjust to different screen sizes and orientations. In this section, we'll explore the concept of fluid grids, how they work, and how to implement them in your web projects.

Understanding Fluid Grids

A fluid grid is a layout system that uses relative units like percentages instead of fixed units like pixels for defining the width of page elements. This approach allows the content to automatically adapt to the available space. It's particularly useful for creating responsive designs because it scales smoothly when viewed on various devices.

Using Percentages for Width

To create a fluid grid layout, you need to use percentages for defining the width of your layout containers and columns. For example, if you want a two-column layout, you can set each column's width to 50% to ensure they take up half of the available space.

```
.column {
    width: 50%;
    float: left;
}
```

In this example, each column will occupy 50% of the parent container's width. When the screen size changes, the columns will automatically adjust to maintain their relative widths.

Media Queries and Breakpoints

Fluid grid layouts are often used in combination with media queries to specify different layouts for different screen sizes or breakpoints. By changing the percentage-based widths at specific breakpoints, you can create layouts that are optimized for various devices.

Here's an example of a simple media query that adjusts the layout for screens with a minimum width of 768 pixels:

```
@media screen and (min-width: 768px) {
    .column {
        width: 33.33%;
    }
}
```

In this case, when the screen width reaches or exceeds 768 pixels, the columns will now take up approximately one-third of the available width.

Handling Gutters and Margins

When working with fluid grids, it's important to consider gutters and margins between columns. You may need to use percentage-based values for gutters and carefully manage margins to ensure a visually appealing layout.

Challenges of Fluid Grids

While fluid grids are powerful for creating responsive layouts, they can be challenging to work with, especially when dealing with complex designs. It's crucial to thoroughly test and refine your layouts across various devices and screen sizes to ensure a consistent and user-friendly experience.

In summary, fluid grid layouts are a fundamental concept in responsive web design. By using percentage-based widths and media queries, you can create layouts that adapt gracefully to different screens and devices, providing an optimal user experience. However, it's important to be mindful of the challenges and complexities involved in working with fluid grids and to continually test your designs for responsiveness.

Section 15.4: Responsive Images

Images play a significant role in web design and content presentation. In responsive web design (RWD), it's essential to ensure that images adapt to various screen sizes and resolutions. This section focuses on responsive images and the techniques to implement them effectively.

Challenges with Fixed-Size Images

Traditional web design often relies on fixed-size images, which can lead to problems on smaller screens or when viewed on devices with different resolutions. Oversized images can result in slower page loading times and unnecessary bandwidth usage. Additionally, images that don't scale well can disrupt the overall layout and user experience.

Using max-width for Images

One common technique for creating responsive images is to set the max-width property of images to 100%. This ensures that images never exceed the width of their container while maintaining their aspect ratio. Here's an example:

```
img {
    max-width: 100%;
    height: auto;
}
```

With this CSS rule, images will scale down proportionally to fit within the width of their parent container, ensuring they look good on both large screens and small mobile devices.

The srcset Attribute

The srcset attribute is an HTML5 feature that allows you to provide multiple image sources based on different device resolutions and screen sizes. Browsers can then choose the most appropriate image source to load, optimizing both performance and visual quality.

```
<img
    src="image-small.jpg"
    srcset="image-small.jpg 480w,
            image-medium.jpg 800w,
            image-large.jpg 1200w"
    alt="Responsive Image"
/>
```

In this example, the browser selects the image source based on the available viewport width and resolution. It will load the most suitable image to prevent unnecessary data transfer.

The sizes Attribute

The `sizes` attribute complements `srcset` by specifying the image's display size in CSS pixels and defining the layout breakpoints. It helps browsers make better decisions about which image to load.

```
<img
    src="image-small.jpg"
    srcset="image-small.jpg 480w,
            image-medium.jpg 800w,
            image-large.jpg 1200w"
    sizes="(max-width: 600px) 100vw, (max-width: 1200px) 50vw, 33vw"
    alt="Responsive Image"
/>
```

In this example, when the viewport is less than 600 pixels wide, the image occupies the full viewport width (`100vw`). When the viewport is between 600 and 1200 pixels wide, the image occupies half the viewport width (`50vw`). For wider viewports, the image takes up one-third of the viewport width (`33vw`).

Art Direction with <picture>

The `<picture>` element allows you to define multiple sources for an image and specify different media conditions and image sources. This is useful when you want to provide different images for different scenarios, such as varying aspect ratios or cropping.

```
<picture>
    <source
        media="(min-width: 800px)"
        srcset="large-image.jpg"
    />
    <img src="default-image.jpg" alt="Responsive Image" />
</picture>
```

In this example, the larger image is displayed only when the viewport width is at least 800 pixels. Otherwise, the default image is shown.

Conclusion

Responsive images are crucial for creating web designs that adapt to a wide range of devices and screen sizes. By using techniques like setting `max-width`, using the `srcset` and `sizes` attributes, and leveraging the `<picture>` element, you can ensure that your images enhance rather than hinder the user experience on all devices.

Section 15.5: Mobile-First Design Approach

In the world of web design, the term "mobile-first" has gained significant traction over the years. It refers to a design philosophy that prioritizes designing for mobile devices before scaling up to larger screens, such as tablets and desktops. This approach has become essential in the era of responsive web design and the increasing prevalence of mobile browsing. In this section, we'll explore the principles of the mobile-first design approach and why it's crucial for modern web development.

The Evolution of Mobile-First

Traditionally, web design began with desktop-first thinking. Websites were primarily designed for large desktop monitors, and then adjustments were made to accommodate smaller screens. However, this approach had several drawbacks:

1. **Slower Load Times**: Desktop-oriented websites often contained large images and complex layouts that took longer to load on mobile devices with limited bandwidth.

2. **Poor User Experience**: Sites not optimized for mobile could be difficult to navigate and read, leading to a subpar user experience.

3. **Lower Search Ranking**: Search engines like Google began penalizing non-mobile-friendly websites in search results.

To address these issues, the mobile-first approach emerged. It encourages designers and developers to start by creating a design tailored specifically for mobile devices. Here's why this approach makes sense:

Benefits of Mobile-First Design

1. **Performance**: Mobile-first designs tend to be more lightweight and optimized for fast loading on mobile networks. This can significantly improve website performance and user satisfaction.

2. **Content Focus**: Designers are forced to prioritize content and features, ensuring that only the most essential elements make it to the mobile version. This helps keep the user's focus on what matters most.

3. **Improved User Experience**: Mobile-first designs are often simpler and more user-friendly. They consider touch-based interactions and smaller screen sizes, leading to a better experience for mobile users.

4. **Search Engine Optimization (SEO)**: Google and other search engines favor mobile-friendly websites in their rankings. A mobile-first approach can positively impact your site's SEO performance.

How to Implement Mobile-First Design

To embrace mobile-first design, consider the following practices:

1. **Start Small**: Begin designing for the smallest screens first, such as smartphones. Define the core features and content needed for a mobile experience.

2. **Progressive Enhancement**: As the screen size increases (e.g., tablet and desktop), add additional features and layout enhancements. This ensures a consistent and optimized experience across devices.

3. **Responsive Design**: Use CSS media queries to apply styles and layout adjustments based on screen size. Test your design thoroughly on various devices and browsers.

4. **Performance Optimization**: Prioritize image optimization, lazy loading, and efficient coding to ensure fast loading times.

5. **User Testing**: Test your design with real users on different devices to gather feedback and make improvements.

Conclusion

Mobile-first design is not just a trend but a best practice in modern web development. Prioritizing mobile users can lead to faster-loading websites, improved user experiences, and higher search engine rankings. By adopting a mobile-first mindset, you can ensure that your web projects are well-prepared for the diverse landscape of devices and screen sizes that users utilize today.

Chapter 16: Cross-Browser Compatibility

Section 16.1: Challenges of Cross-Browser Compatibility

Cross-browser compatibility is a critical aspect of web development. It refers to the ability of a website or web application to function consistently and correctly across different web browsers. While modern web standards have improved browser compatibility, challenges still exist due to variations in rendering engines, browser versions, and user preferences. In this section, we'll explore the challenges posed by cross-browser compatibility and strategies to overcome them.

The Browser Landscape

The web browser ecosystem is diverse, with several popular browsers available across multiple platforms. Some of the major players include Google Chrome, Mozilla Firefox, Apple Safari, Microsoft Edge, and Opera. Each of these browsers may use a different rendering engine to display web content.

Key Challenges

1. **Rendering Engines**: Browsers use different rendering engines, such as Blink (used by Chrome), Gecko (used by Firefox), and WebKit (used by Safari). These engines may interpret HTML, CSS, and JavaScript differently, leading to inconsistent rendering of web pages.

2. **Browser Versions**: Browsers receive regular updates, introducing new features and improvements. However, older versions of browsers may lack support for modern web technologies, requiring developers to consider backward compatibility.

3. **Vendor-Specific Prefixes**: In the past, browsers implemented experimental CSS properties with vendor-specific prefixes (e.g., `-webkit-`, `-moz-`, `-ms-`). While these prefixes are less common today, they can still cause issues on older browsers.

4. **JavaScript Compatibility**: JavaScript code can behave differently across browsers due to variations in how they interpret and execute code. Developers need to test and adapt their scripts for cross-browser compatibility.

5. **CSS Flexibility**: CSS layout techniques like Flexbox and Grid may require vendor-specific properties in older browsers. Handling these differences is crucial for consistent layouts.

Strategies for Cross-Browser Compatibility

To address these challenges and ensure cross-browser compatibility, consider the following strategies:

1. **Use Modern Web Standards**: Follow web standards and use HTML, CSS, and JavaScript features that are well-supported across all modern browsers.

2. **Progressive Enhancement**: Start with a basic, functional version of your website and progressively enhance it with advanced features for modern browsers while maintaining core functionality on older ones.

3. **Feature Detection**: Use feature detection libraries like Modernizr or write custom JavaScript to check for browser support and provide fallbacks or alternative experiences when necessary.

4. **Testing and Debugging**: Regularly test your website on various browsers and browser versions. Use developer tools to identify and fix compatibility issues.

5. **Polyfills**: Implement JavaScript polyfills or libraries like Babel to bring modern features to older browsers.

6. **CSS Prefixes**: Minimize the use of vendor-specific CSS prefixes. When needed, use tools like Autoprefixer to automatically add prefixes during the build process.

7. **User-Agent Sniffing**: While not recommended, you can detect the user's browser and version using the User-Agent string and apply specific fixes or workarounds.

Conclusion

Cross-browser compatibility remains a challenge in web development, but it's a crucial aspect of delivering a seamless user experience. By following best practices, testing rigorously, and using appropriate strategies, developers can ensure that their websites and web applications work well across a wide range of browsers, enhancing accessibility and user satisfaction.

Section 16.2: Browser Testing Tools

Testing your web applications and websites across different browsers and browser versions is a crucial step in achieving cross-browser compatibility. Fortunately, there are several browser testing tools and services available to help streamline this process. In this section, we'll explore some of the popular tools that can assist you in testing and debugging your web projects for cross-browser compatibility.

1. Browser Developer Tools

Most modern web browsers come equipped with built-in developer tools. These tools are invaluable for debugging and testing web pages. They allow you to inspect the HTML, CSS, and JavaScript of a page, modify the DOM (Document Object Model), analyze network requests, and emulate different devices and browser versions. Here are some key developer tools:

- **Google Chrome DevTools**: Press Ctrl + Shift + I (or Cmd + Option + I on Mac) to open Chrome's DevTools. It includes a variety of panels for inspecting and debugging your web pages.

- **Mozilla Firefox DevTools**: Access Firefox's DevTools by pressing `Ctrl + Shift + I` (or `Cmd + Option + I` on Mac). It provides similar functionality to Chrome DevTools.

- **Microsoft Edge DevTools**: In the Edge browser, press `F12` to open DevTools. Edge DevTools offer debugging capabilities similar to those in Chrome and Firefox.

- **Safari Web Inspector**: On Safari, go to `Safari > Preferences > Advanced` and enable the "Show Develop menu in menu bar" option. Then, you can open the Web Inspector from the Develop menu.

2. Cross-Browser Testing Platforms

Several online platforms offer comprehensive cross-browser testing services. These platforms allow you to test your web pages on a wide range of browsers and operating systems without having to maintain physical devices. Some popular options include:

- **Sauce Labs**: Sauce Labs provides a cloud-based platform for testing web and mobile applications on various browsers and devices. It offers real-time testing and automated testing options.

- **BrowserStack**: BrowserStack offers a similar service, enabling you to test your websites on a wide array of browsers, including mobile and desktop browsers, as well as different operating systems.

- **CrossBrowserTesting**: This platform provides interactive testing, automated testing, and visual testing for cross-browser compatibility. It also offers integrations with popular testing frameworks.

3. Browser Extensions and Add-Ons

Several browser extensions and add-ons can simplify cross-browser testing directly from your browser. For example:

- **IE Tab**: This extension for Chrome and Firefox allows you to view web pages using the Internet Explorer rendering engine, which can be helpful for testing compatibility with older versions of Internet Explorer.

- **User-Agent Switchers**: Extensions like "User-Agent Switcher" for Chrome and Firefox let you change your browser's user agent string to emulate different browsers and devices.

4. Online Testing Tools

There are web-based tools that offer quick and simple browser testing:

- **LambdaTest**: LambdaTest allows you to perform live interactive testing on various browsers and platforms. It also offers screenshot testing and automation.

- **Browsershots**: Browsershots is a free online service that generates screenshots of your website on multiple browsers running on different operating systems.

5. Virtual Machines and Emulators

For more extensive testing, you can use virtual machines and emulators to run different operating systems and browsers on your development machine. This approach provides a more accurate representation of how your site behaves on various platforms.

- **VirtualBox**: VirtualBox is a free and open-source virtualization software that allows you to run multiple virtual machines with different browser configurations.

- **Android Emulator**: If you're targeting mobile devices, the Android Emulator, which is part of the Android Studio development environment, can emulate various Android devices and versions.

Conclusion

Cross-browser testing tools and services are essential for ensuring that your web projects work correctly and consistently across different browsers and devices. Whether you choose built-in developer tools, online platforms, or virtualization solutions, investing time in thorough testing is critical to delivering a seamless user experience and maintaining cross-browser compatibility.

Section 16.3: CSS Vendor Prefixes

CSS vendor prefixes, also known as browser prefixes or CSS browser-specific prefixes, are a set of special prefixes added to CSS property names to implement experimental or non-standard CSS features in web browsers. These prefixes were initially introduced to allow web developers to experiment with new CSS properties and features before they became part of the official CSS specification. While they were once necessary, their usage has declined significantly in recent years due to advancements in web standards and browser compatibility.

The History of Vendor Prefixes

Vendor prefixes were introduced as a way for browser vendors to implement and test experimental CSS features without risking conflicts with other browser vendors or the final CSS specification. Each vendor would use its own prefix to indicate that a particular CSS property or feature was experimental and subject to change.

For example, here are some common vendor prefixes:

- `-webkit-` (used by WebKit-based browsers like Safari and early versions of Chrome)
- `-moz-` (used by Mozilla Firefox)
- `-ms-` (used by Microsoft Internet Explorer and Microsoft Edge)

- -o- (used by Opera)

Web developers would include these prefixes in their CSS code to target specific browsers. For instance, to apply a CSS rule only to WebKit-based browsers, you might use `-webkit-transform`.

While vendor prefixes served their purpose by allowing early experimentation, they introduced several issues:

1. **Browser-Specific Code**: Developers had to write and maintain multiple versions of their CSS rules to support different browsers, which increased code complexity.

2. **Fragmented Codebase**: The use of vendor prefixes created a fragmented codebase, making CSS harder to read and maintain.

3. **Maintenance Challenges**: As web standards evolved, some browsers dropped support for old prefixes, while others introduced new ones. This made it challenging to keep CSS code up-to-date.

4. **Non-Standard Features**: Using vendor prefixes often meant relying on non-standard CSS features that might never become part of the official specification.

In recent years, the use of vendor prefixes has significantly declined for several reasons:

1. **Standardization**: Many experimental CSS features that once required vendor prefixes have now been standardized and integrated into the official CSS specification.

2. **Autoprefixer**: Tools like Autoprefixer have gained popularity, automatically adding necessary prefixes based on your desired browser support. This reduces the need for manual prefixing in your CSS.

3. **Browser Support**: Modern web browsers aim to be more standards-compliant and provide better cross-browser compatibility. They are less reliant on non-standard features.

While vendor prefixes are mostly obsolete today, there are a few best practices to consider:

1. **Use Autoprefixer**: Incorporate Autoprefixer into your build process to handle prefixing automatically. It ensures that your CSS remains compatible with older browsers.

2. **Avoid New Prefixes**: Avoid using new or experimental prefixes, as they are unlikely to be widely supported. Instead, focus on standard CSS properties and features.

3. **Check Browser Compatibility**: Regularly test your website or web app in various browsers to ensure compatibility and identify any issues that may arise.

4. **Update Legacy Code**: If you have legacy code with vendor prefixes, consider updating it to use standard CSS properties where applicable.

In summary, while vendor prefixes played a role in the history of web development, their use has become less relevant due to the evolution of web standards and improved browser compatibility. Modern web development practices prioritize standardized CSS properties and automatic prefixing tools to ensure cross-browser compatibility.

Section 16.4: JavaScript Compatibility

Ensuring JavaScript compatibility across different web browsers is a crucial aspect of web development. JavaScript is a versatile and widely used programming language for building dynamic and interactive web applications. However, due to variations in browser implementations and JavaScript engine versions, developers often encounter compatibility issues. In this section, we'll explore the challenges of JavaScript compatibility and best practices to mitigate them.

Challenges of JavaScript Compatibility

1. **Browser Differences**: Different web browsers (e.g., Chrome, Firefox, Safari, Internet Explorer, Edge) may interpret JavaScript code differently. What works in one browser may not work the same way in another.

2. **Browser Versions**: Even within the same browser, different versions of JavaScript engines may have varying levels of support for language features and APIs. Older browsers may lack support for modern JavaScript features.

3. **ES5 vs. ES6+**: JavaScript has undergone significant updates, such as ECMAScript 6 (ES6) and later versions. While modern browsers support these updates, older browsers may not. Developers need to consider backward compatibility.

4. **Feature Detection**: Feature detection is essential to determine whether a specific JavaScript feature or API is supported by the user's browser. This prevents errors and ensures graceful degradation.

5. **Polyfills**: To address compatibility gaps, developers often use polyfills—JavaScript code that provides missing features in older browsers. Polyfills enable the use of modern JavaScript features while maintaining compatibility.

Best Practices for JavaScript Compatibility

1. **Use Feature Detection**: Employ feature detection techniques to check if a specific JavaScript feature or API is supported before using it. Libraries like Modernizr can help with feature detection.

```javascript
if (typeof window.localStorage !== 'undefined') {
  // Use LocalStorage
} else {
  // Handle without LocalStorage
}
```

2. **Progressive Enhancement**: Build your web application with progressive enhancement in mind. Start with a core functionality that works on all browsers and then add advanced features for modern browsers.

3. **Transpilation**: Use a JavaScript transpiler like Babel to convert modern JavaScript code (ES6+) into older versions (ES5) that are compatible with a wider range of browsers. This allows you to write modern code while ensuring broad support.

```javascript
// ES6 code
const greet = (name) => `Hello, ${name}!`;

// Transpiled to ES5
var greet = function (name) {
  return 'Hello, ' + name + '!';
};
```

4. **Polyfills and Shims**: Include polyfills for missing features or APIs. Libraries like "core-js" and "polyfill.io" can automatically load polyfills based on the user's browser.

5. **Regular Testing**: Continuously test your web application in different browsers and browser versions. Automated testing tools like Selenium and cross-browser testing services can help identify compatibility issues.

6. **User-Agent Detection**: While not recommended as the primary method, you can use user-agent detection as a last resort to handle specific browser quirks. However, this approach is error-prone and less maintainable.

```javascript
if (navigator.userAgent.indexOf('MSIE') !== -1) {
  // Handle Internet Explorer
}
```

7. **Stay Informed**: Keep up with JavaScript language updates, browser releases, and compatibility changes. The web development community often shares solutions and best practices for common compatibility issues.

In conclusion, achieving JavaScript compatibility across various web browsers is essential for delivering a consistent user experience. By using feature detection, progressive enhancement, transpilation, polyfills, and thorough testing, developers can navigate the challenges of JavaScript compatibility and ensure their web applications work seamlessly on a wide range of devices and browsers.

Section 16.5: Graceful Degradation and Progressive Enhancement

Graceful degradation and progressive enhancement are two fundamental principles in web development that address the challenge of providing a consistent user experience across different web browsers and devices. These concepts revolve around building web applications that work well in modern environments while still being functional in less capable or older environments.

Graceful Degradation

Graceful degradation is an approach where you start by developing a web application or website with all the bells and whistles, taking advantage of the latest web technologies and features. However, you also acknowledge that not all users will have access to the same technology stack.

In the context of graceful degradation:

1. **Focus on Modern Browsers**: Your primary goal is to deliver the best experience to users with modern web browsers that support the latest standards, features, and performance improvements.

2. **Identify Essential Functionality**: Identify the core functionality of your application that should be preserved even in older or less capable browsers. These are the features that are critical for users to accomplish their tasks.

3. **Fallbacks for Older Browsers**: Implement fallback mechanisms for older browsers. This may involve using simpler JavaScript, CSS, or HTML to provide a basic level of functionality. While it won't be as feature-rich as the modern version, it should be usable.

4. **Testing Across Environments**: Thoroughly test your application in different browsers and browser versions to ensure that it gracefully degrades without breaking. Automated testing tools and services can be valuable for this purpose.

Here's an example of graceful degradation using JavaScript:

```javascript
// Modern browsers
if (typeof fetch !== 'undefined') {
  fetch('/api/data')
    .then(response => response.json())
    .then(data => {
      // Process data for modern browsers
    })
    .catch(error => {
      // Handle errors for modern browsers
    });
}
// Fallback for older browsers (e.g., using XMLHttpRequest)
```

```
else {
  var xhr = new XMLHttpRequest();
  xhr.open('GET', '/api/data', true);
  xhr.onreadystatechange = function () {
    if (xhr.readyState === 4 && xhr.status === 200) {
      var data = JSON.parse(xhr.responseText);
      // Process data for older browsers
    }
  };
  xhr.send();
}
```

Progressive Enhancement

Progressive enhancement, on the other hand, takes a different approach:

1. **Start with a Solid Foundation**: Begin by creating a baseline version of your web application that is functional in all web browsers, including older ones. This baseline should use standard HTML and CSS without relying on advanced JavaScript or cutting-edge features.

2. **Enhance for Modern Browsers**: Once the basic version is working, progressively enhance the user experience for modern browsers by adding advanced features, interactivity, and optimizations. This is where you leverage technologies like JavaScript frameworks, CSS3, and HTML5.

3. **Feature Detection**: Use feature detection to check if a particular browser supports a specific feature before applying it. If the feature is supported, enhance the user experience accordingly. If not, users still get a functional experience.

Here's an example of progressive enhancement:

```
<!-- Baseline HTML for all browsers -->
<button id="myButton">Click Me</button>

<!-- Progressive enhancement with JavaScript -->
<script>
  if (document.querySelector && 'addEventListener' in window) {
    var button = document.querySelector('#myButton');
    button.addEventListener('click', function () {
      alert('Button clicked!');
    });
  }
</script>
```

In this example, the baseline HTML includes a simple button element that works in all browsers. The JavaScript code then progressively enhances the button's functionality by adding a click event listener for modern browsers.

Both graceful degradation and progressive enhancement strategies are valuable in web development, and the choice between them depends on your target audience, project requirements, and development approach. Ultimately, these principles help ensure that your web applications are accessible and usable across a wide range of devices and browsers, delivering a consistent experience to all users.

Chapter 17: HTML5 and Modern Web Features

Section 17.1: HTML5 Features Overview

HTML5, the fifth major version of the Hypertext Markup Language, has brought significant advancements to web development since its introduction. It has introduced a wide array of features, elements, and APIs that have transformed how web applications are built and experienced. In this section, we will provide an overview of some key HTML5 features that have had a substantial impact on the modern web.

1. Semantic Elements: HTML5 introduced several new semantic elements like `<header>`, `<nav>`, `<footer>`, and `<article>`. These elements provide a more meaningful structure to web documents, making it easier for search engines and assistive technologies to understand the content.

2. Audio and Video Support: HTML5 includes native support for embedding audio and video content using the `<audio>` and `<video>` elements. This eliminates the need for third-party plugins like Adobe Flash and simplifies multimedia integration.

```
<video controls>
  <source src="movie.mp4" type="video/mp4">
  <source src="movie.webm" type="video/webm">
  Your browser does not support the video tag.
</video>
```

3. Canvas: The `<canvas>` element enables dynamic rendering of graphics and animations using JavaScript. It has given rise to a wide range of web-based games, interactive visualizations, and drawing applications.

```
<canvas id="myCanvas" width="400" height="200"></canvas>
<script>
  var canvas = document.getElementById("myCanvas");
  var ctx = canvas.getContext("2d");
  // Drawing operations using JavaScript
</script>
```

4. Local Storage: The Web Storage API, including `localStorage` and `sessionStorage`, allows web applications to store data locally on the user's device. This feature is handy for building offline-capable web apps and caching resources.

```
// Storing data in LocalStorage
localStorage.setItem("username", "john_doe");
// Retrieving data from LocalStorage
var username = localStorage.getItem("username");
```

5. Web Workers: HTML5 introduced web workers, which are background scripts that can run concurrently with the main JavaScript thread. They are often used for tasks that require significant processing power without blocking the user interface.

```javascript
// Creating a web worker
var worker = new Worker("myWorker.js");
// Handling messages from the worker
worker.onmessage = function (event) {
  console.log("Message from worker: " + event.data);
};
```

6. Geolocation: With the Geolocation API, web applications can access a user's geographical location. This feature is utilized in various location-based services and mapping applications.

```javascript
// Getting user's current location
navigator.geolocation.getCurrentPosition(function (position) {
  var latitude = position.coords.latitude;
  var longitude = position.coords.longitude;
  console.log("Latitude: " + latitude + ", Longitude: " + longitude);
});
```

7. Offline Web Applications: HTML5 introduced the Application Cache (AppCache) API, allowing web apps to work offline. Developers can specify which resources to cache, ensuring that the app remains functional even without an internet connection.

```html
<!-- Adding a manifest attribute to specify the cache manifest file -->
<html manifest="myapp.appcache">
  <!-- Your web app content -->
</html>
```

These are just a few highlights of HTML5 features. HTML5 has revolutionized web development by providing a richer set of tools and capabilities for creating modern, interactive, and responsive web applications. As the web continues to evolve, HTML5 remains a foundation for building innovative digital experiences.

Section 17.2: Geolocation and Web Storage

HTML5 introduced a set of powerful APIs that enhance the capabilities of web applications. In this section, we will explore two essential HTML5 features: Geolocation and Web Storage.

Geolocation API

The Geolocation API allows web applications to access a user's geographical location through their device. This feature has led to the development of various location-based services and applications. To use the Geolocation API, you can follow these steps:

1. **Check for Geolocation Support**: Before using geolocation, it's essential to verify if the user's browser supports this feature.

```
if ("geolocation" in navigator) {
  // Geolocation is available
} else {
  // Geolocation is not available
}
```

2. **Get the User's Current Position**: To retrieve the user's current position, you can use the `getCurrentPosition` method. It takes two callback functions as parameters, one for success and another for error handling.

```
navigator.geolocation.getCurrentPosition(
  function (position) {
    var latitude = position.coords.latitude;
    var longitude = position.coords.longitude;
    console.log("Latitude: " + latitude + ", Longitude: " + longitude);
  },
  function (error) {
    console.error("Error getting location: " + error.message);
  }
);
```

3. **Watch for Changes in Position**: If you need continuous updates of the user's location, you can use the `watchPosition` method. It works similarly to `getCurrentPosition` but continues to monitor changes.

```
var watchId = navigator.geolocation.watchPosition(
  function (position) {
    var latitude = position.coords.latitude;
    var longitude = position.coords.longitude;
    console.log("Updated Latitude: " + latitude + ", Longitude: " + longitude
);
  },
  function (error) {
    console.error("Error getting location: " + error.message);
  }
);
```

4. **Clear Watch**: To stop watching the user's position, you can use the `clearWatch` method and pass the `watchId` obtained from `watchPosition`.

```
navigator.geolocation.clearWatch(watchId);
```

Web Storage

Web Storage provides a way for web applications to store data locally on the user's device. It offers two mechanisms: `localStorage` and `sessionStorage`.

1. **localStorage**: Data stored in `localStorage` persists even after the browser is closed. It is useful for storing user preferences, login tokens, or any data that should be available across sessions.

```
// Storing data in LocalStorage
localStorage.setItem("username", "john_doe");
```

```
// Retrieving data from LocalStorage
var username = localStorage.getItem("username");
```

2. **sessionStorage**: Data stored in sessionStorage is only available for the duration of the page session. Once the user closes the tab or browser, the data is cleared.

```
// Storing data in sessionStorage
sessionStorage.setItem("theme", "dark");
// Retrieving data from sessionStorage
var theme = sessionStorage.getItem("theme");
```

Both localStorage and sessionStorage use a simple key-value pair system for storing data. They have a limit of around 5-10 MB of storage per domain, and the data is stored as strings.

These HTML5 features, Geolocation and Web Storage, have greatly enriched web application development, enabling developers to create more interactive and personalized experiences for users.

Section 17.3: Web Workers and APIs

Web Workers and APIs are essential components of modern web development that allow developers to perform tasks concurrently, enhancing the user experience and enabling more complex web applications.

Web Workers

Web Workers are a JavaScript feature that allows you to run scripts in the background, separate from the main UI thread. This separation prevents long-running tasks from freezing the user interface, ensuring a smoother browsing experience. Web Workers are commonly used for tasks such as complex calculations, data processing, or even running a WebSocket connection.

Here's how you can create and use a Web Worker:

```
// Creating a Web Worker
const worker = new Worker('worker.js');

// Sending data to the Web Worker
worker.postMessage({ message: 'Hello, Worker!' });

// Handling messages from the Web Worker
worker.onmessage = (event) => {
  console.log('Message from Worker:', event.data);
};

// Terminating the Web Worker
worker.terminate();
```

In the example above, we create a Web Worker from an external script file called `worker.js`. We send a message to the worker, and when it responds, we handle the message using the `onmessage` event handler. Finally, we terminate the worker when it's no longer needed.

APIs (Application Programming Interfaces)

APIs are sets of rules and protocols that allow different software applications to communicate with each other. In web development, APIs are commonly used to access external services or data sources. Some of the most commonly used web APIs include:

1. **Fetch API**: The Fetch API is used to make network requests (e.g., fetching data from a server) and handle responses. It provides a more modern and flexible alternative to the older XMLHttpRequest.

```
fetch('https://api.example.com/data')
  .then((response) => response.json())
  .then((data) => {
    console.log(data);
  })
  .catch((error) => {
    console.error('Error:', error);
  });
```

2. **WebSockets**: WebSockets provide a full-duplex communication channel over a single TCP connection, enabling real-time, bidirectional communication between the client and server. They are commonly used in online gaming, chat applications, and collaborative tools.

```
const socket = new WebSocket('wss://socket.example.com');

socket.addEventListener('open', (event) => {
  // Connection opened
});

socket.addEventListener('message', (event) => {
  // Received a message from the server
  console.log('Message from server:', event.data);
});

socket.addEventListener('close', (event) => {
  // Connection closed
});
```

3. **Geolocation API**: As mentioned in the previous section, the Geolocation API allows web applications to access a user's geographical location, enabling location-based services and applications.

4. **IndexedDB**: IndexedDB is an API for storing structured data on the client-side, providing a more powerful and versatile way to manage data than Web Storage.

These are just a few examples of the many APIs available for web developers. Each API serves a specific purpose and can greatly extend the functionality of web applications. When using APIs, it's essential to review their documentation to understand their capabilities and how to use them effectively in your projects.

In summary, Web Workers and APIs are crucial tools in modern web development, allowing developers to create responsive and feature-rich web applications. Web Workers enable parallel processing, while APIs provide access to external services and data sources, expanding the possibilities for web-based applications.

Section 17.4: Offline Web Applications

Offline web applications are a crucial aspect of modern web development, as they allow users to access web content and applications even when they are not connected to the internet. This feature improves the user experience and ensures that web applications remain functional in various scenarios, such as in areas with poor connectivity or during temporary network outages.

Service Workers

Service Workers are a fundamental technology for building offline web applications. They are JavaScript files that run in the background, separate from the web page, and act as a proxy between the web application and the network. Service Workers intercept network requests and can cache resources to enable offline access. Here's a high-level overview of how Service Workers work:

1. **Registration**: To use a Service Worker, it needs to be registered in your web application. This typically happens in your main JavaScript file.

    ```javascript
    if ('serviceWorker' in navigator) {
      navigator.serviceWorker.register('/service-worker.js')
        .then((registration) => {
          console.log('Service Worker registered:', registration);
        })
        .catch((error) => {
          console.error('Service Worker registration failed:', error);
        });
    }
    ```

2. **Service Worker File**: The Service Worker script (`service-worker.js`) contains logic for intercepting and handling network requests and caching resources.

    ```javascript
    self.addEventListener('fetch', (event) => {
      // Intercept network requests and respond with cached resources
      event.respondWith(
        caches.match(event.request).then((response) => {
          return response || fetch(event.request);
    ```

```
      })
    );
  });
```

3. **Caching**: Service Workers can cache static assets, such as HTML, CSS, JavaScript, and images, as well as dynamic data from API requests. This cached data is stored locally on the user's device.

4. **Offline Experience**: When a user visits your web application while online, the Service Worker caches resources as they are requested. When the user goes offline, the Service Worker can intercept network requests and respond with cached resources, providing a seamless offline experience.

5. **Background Sync**: Service Workers can also enable background synchronization, allowing data to be sent to the server when the user is back online.

Web Storage

In addition to Service Workers, web developers can utilize web storage mechanisms like the **Web Storage API** (localStorage and sessionStorage) and the **IndexedDB API** to store data locally in the user's browser. These storage options enable the caching of data, user preferences, and even entire application states for offline use.

- **localStorage**: Allows you to store key-value pairs persistently in the user's browser. Data stored in localStorage remains even after the browser is closed and can be accessed across sessions.

  ```
  localStorage.setItem('username', 'john_doe');
  const username = localStorage.getItem('username');
  ```

- **sessionStorage**: Similar to localStorage, but data stored in sessionStorage is only available for the duration of a single page session. It is cleared when the user closes the browser tab.

  ```
  sessionStorage.setItem('theme', 'dark');
  const theme = sessionStorage.getItem('theme');
  ```

- **IndexedDB**: A more advanced client-side database system that provides structured storage for complex data. It allows developers to create, read, update, and delete data, making it suitable for applications with significant offline data requirements.

  ```
  // Open or create a database
  const db = indexedDB.open('myDatabase', 1);

  // Define object stores and perform database operations
  db.onsuccess = (event) => {
    const database = event.target.result;
    const transaction = database.transaction('contacts', 'readwrite');
    const objectStore = transaction.objectStore('contacts');
  ```

```
// Add data
objectStore.add({ name: 'John Doe', email: 'john@example.com' });

// Query data
const getRequest = objectStore.get(1);
getRequest.onsuccess = (event) => {
  const contact = event.target.result;
  console.log('Contact:', contact);
};

// Update data
const updateRequest = objectStore.put({ name: 'Jane Doe', email: 'jan
e@example.com' }, 1);

// Delete data
const deleteRequest = objectStore.delete(1);
};
```

By combining Service Workers with web storage options like localStorage, sessionStorage, and IndexedDB, web developers can create web applications that provide reliable offline access to content and data, delivering a seamless user experience in various network conditions. This capability is particularly valuable for progressive web apps (PWAs) and other web applications where offline functionality is essential.

Section 17.5: Enhancing User Experience

Enhancing the user experience is a fundamental goal in web development. To create successful websites and web applications, it's essential to prioritize user experience (UX) by implementing various techniques and best practices. In this section, we'll explore key strategies for improving UX.

1. Responsive Design

Responsive web design is an approach that ensures websites and web applications adapt to different screen sizes and devices. This includes desktop computers, laptops, tablets, and smartphones. By using responsive design techniques, you can provide a consistent and user-friendly experience across a wide range of devices.

Key components of responsive design include:

- **Media Queries**: CSS media queries allow you to apply different styles based on screen size, orientation, and other characteristics.

```
@media (max-width: 768px) {
  /* Styles for screens smaller than 768px wide */
}
```

- **Fluid Grids**: Use fluid grid layouts that automatically adjust the width and positioning of elements based on screen size.

- **Flexible Images**: Ensure that images scale proportionally to fit various screen sizes without distortion.

2. Performance Optimization

Website speed and performance significantly impact user experience. Slow-loading websites can lead to high bounce rates and user frustration. To optimize performance:

- **Minimize HTTP Requests**: Reduce the number of HTTP requests by combining and minifying CSS and JavaScript files.

- **Optimize Images**: Compress and serve images in modern formats (e.g., WebP) to reduce file sizes.

- **Lazy Loading**: Implement lazy loading for images and other non-essential resources, loading them only when they come into the user's viewport.

- **Content Delivery Networks (CDNs)**: Use CDNs to distribute content to servers located closer to the user, reducing latency.

3. Usability and Accessibility

Usability and accessibility are critical aspects of UX:

- **Usability Testing**: Conduct usability testing to gather feedback from users and identify areas for improvement in terms of navigation, content layout, and interaction design.

- **Accessibility**: Ensure your website or application is accessible to all users, including those with disabilities. Follow web accessibility standards (WCAG) to provide an inclusive experience.

4. Mobile-First Design

With the increasing use of mobile devices, adopting a mobile-first design approach is beneficial. Start by designing for mobile screens and then progressively enhance for larger screens. This approach ensures that mobile users have a smooth experience.

5. Clear Navigation and Information Architecture

Well-organized navigation and information architecture make it easier for users to find what they're looking for. Use clear and concise menus, breadcrumbs, and logical content hierarchies.

6. Consistency in Design and Branding

Maintaining consistency in design, branding, and user interface elements across your website or application establishes trust and helps users navigate with confidence.

7. Feedback and Error Handling

Provide feedback to users when they perform actions, such as submitting forms or making selections. Additionally, offer clear error messages and guidance on how to correct issues.

8. Content Quality

High-quality, relevant content is essential for user engagement. Ensure that your content is well-written, informative, and up to date.

9. Mobile App-Like Interactions

Web applications can offer app-like interactions by incorporating smooth transitions, gestures, and animations. This creates a more engaging and enjoyable experience.

10. Security and Privacy

Protect user data and privacy by implementing strong security measures, such as HTTPS, and providing transparent information about data usage and privacy policies.

By focusing on these strategies and continuously seeking user feedback, you can create web experiences that delight users, keep them engaged, and encourage them to return to your site or application. Prioritizing user experience not only benefits your audience but can also lead to higher conversion rates and user loyalty.

Chapter 18: Web Accessibility and SEO

Section 18.1: Accessibility Standards and Guidelines

Web accessibility is the practice of ensuring that websites and web applications are usable by people with disabilities. Accessibility is not only a legal requirement in many regions but also a fundamental aspect of designing inclusive and user-friendly digital experiences. In this section, we'll explore accessibility standards and guidelines that web developers should be aware of when creating web content.

1. Web Content Accessibility Guidelines (WCAG)

The Web Content Accessibility Guidelines (WCAG) are a set of internationally recognized standards developed by the World Wide Web Consortium (W3C). WCAG provides a comprehensive framework for making web content more accessible to individuals with disabilities. These guidelines are organized into four principles:

- **Perceivable**: Information and user interface components must be presented in a way that users can perceive, such as providing text alternatives for non-text content.

- **Operable**: User interface components and navigation must be operable, including keyboard accessibility and predictable user interactions.

- **Understandable**: Information and operation of the user interface must be understandable, with clear and consistent navigation and labeling.

- **Robust**: Content must be robust enough to be reliably interpreted by a wide variety of user agents, including assistive technologies.

2. Section 508

In the United States, Section 508 of the Rehabilitation Act mandates that federal agencies' electronic and information technology be accessible to people with disabilities. This includes websites, software, and hardware. Section 508 adopts the WCAG guidelines as the standard for web accessibility.

3. Americans with Disabilities Act (ADA)

The Americans with Disabilities Act (ADA) is a civil rights law in the United States that prohibits discrimination against people with disabilities. While the ADA doesn't explicitly mention web accessibility, it has been interpreted by courts to apply to websites and digital content. Many lawsuits have been filed against organizations for inaccessible websites under the ADA.

4. EU Web Accessibility Directive

In the European Union, the Web Accessibility Directive requires public sector websites and mobile applications to be accessible. It references the WCAG 2.1 AA standard as the benchmark for accessibility compliance.

5. Accessible Rich Internet Applications (ARIA)

ARIA is a set of attributes that can be added to HTML elements to provide additional information to assistive technologies. ARIA is particularly useful for making dynamic web content, such as web applications, more accessible. It helps convey roles, states, properties, and relationships in a way that can be understood by screen readers.

6. Testing and Evaluation Tools

Numerous tools are available to help developers test and evaluate the accessibility of their websites. These tools include automated scanners, browser extensions, and screen reader software for manual testing.

7. Inclusive Design

In addition to adhering to guidelines, practicing inclusive design involves considering the needs of all users from the outset of a project. This approach fosters a culture of accessibility and ensures that accessibility is integrated into the design and development process.

8. Benefits of Web Accessibility

Web accessibility not only helps people with disabilities but also benefits a broader audience. It improves usability, enhances search engine optimization (SEO), and increases the potential audience and customer base for websites.

9. Continuous Improvement

Web accessibility is an ongoing process. Regular audits, testing, and updates are essential to maintaining accessibility compliance, especially as websites evolve over time.

By following accessibility standards and guidelines, web developers can create digital content that is welcoming and usable by everyone, regardless of their abilities or disabilities. This not only promotes inclusivity but also helps organizations avoid legal issues and reach a wider audience.

Section 18.2: Creating Accessible Content

Ensuring web accessibility is not only a legal requirement but also a moral and practical obligation for web developers. In this section, we will explore the principles and best practices for creating accessible content that can be used by people with various disabilities.

1. Semantic HTML

Semantic HTML elements play a crucial role in making web content accessible. Using appropriate tags for headings, lists, links, and form elements provides a structured and meaningful hierarchy that can be interpreted by assistive technologies like screen readers. Here are some key semantic HTML elements and their purposes:

- `<h1>`, `<h2>`, `<h3>`, etc.: Use these for headings and subheadings to structure your content logically.

- `<ul>`, `<ol>`, `<li>`: For creating unordered and ordered lists.

- `<a>`: Use the anchor tag for hyperlinks. Provide descriptive link text that makes sense out of context.

- `<button>`: Use for clickable buttons or interactive elements.

- `<input>`, `<label>`, `<textarea>`: For form elements, use labels to describe the purpose of input fields.

2. Alternative Text for Images

Images should have descriptive alternative text (alt text) that conveys their content and purpose. Alt text is essential for users who cannot see images. Be concise but descriptive in your alt text. For example, `<img src="cat.jpg" alt="A black and white cat playing with a toy mouse">`.

3. Keyboard Navigation

Ensure that all interactive elements, such as links, buttons, and form fields, can be accessed and operated using only the keyboard. This is vital for users who cannot use a mouse or other pointing devices.

4. Focus Styles

Make sure that focus indicators are visible and distinct. Users who navigate with the keyboard rely on these focus styles to know which element is currently active. Avoid removing or hiding focus styles unless you provide an alternative method for keyboard users.

5. Color Contrast

Ensure there is sufficient color contrast between text and its background to make content readable for users with visual impairments. WCAG provides specific guidelines for contrast ratios. You can use online tools to check contrast levels.

6. Video and Audio Accessibility

For multimedia content, provide captions for videos and transcripts for audio files. This ensures that users with hearing impairments can access the content. Also, provide options to pause or stop auto-playing media.

7. Forms and Error Handling

In forms, use clear and concise labels. Provide informative error messages when users make mistakes. Ensure that error messages are associated with the corresponding form fields and are announced by screen readers.

8. Testing with Assistive Technologies

Regularly test your website using screen readers, keyboard navigation, and other assistive technologies. This helps identify and address accessibility issues.

9. ARIA Roles and Attributes

Accessible Rich Internet Applications (ARIA) attributes can be used to enhance the accessibility of dynamic web content. Roles like "button," "menu," or "alert" help convey the purpose of elements to screen readers.

10. Responsive Design

Ensure that your website is responsive and adapts to different screen sizes. Users with disabilities may rely on various devices and screen sizes, so a responsive design ensures usability for a broader audience.

11. User Testing

Involve users with disabilities in user testing and gather feedback to improve your site's accessibility. Their insights are invaluable for identifying and addressing real-world accessibility challenges.

Creating accessible content is an ongoing commitment. By following these best practices, web developers can make their websites and web applications more inclusive, providing a better experience for all users, regardless of their abilities or disabilities.

Section 18.3: ARIA Roles and Attributes

Accessible Rich Internet Applications (ARIA) is a set of attributes that can be added to HTML elements to enhance the accessibility of dynamic content, especially in web applications. ARIA roles and attributes provide additional information to assistive technologies like screen readers, making it easier for users with disabilities to navigate and interact with web content.

1. ARIA Roles

ARIA roles define the purpose or role of an element on a web page. Here are some common ARIA roles:

- `role="button"`: Indicates that an element is interactive and behaves like a button.

- `role="link"`: Indicates that an element is a hyperlink or behaves like one.

- `role="menu"`: Used to define a menu widget, such as a dropdown menu.

- `role="list"`: Indicates a list of items.

- `role="listitem"`: Specifies an item within a list.

- `role="checkbox"`: Used for checkboxes or elements that behave like checkboxes.

- `role="radio"`: Indicates a radio button or elements that behave like radio buttons.

- `role="dialog"`: Represents a dialog or modal window.

- `role="alert"`: Indicates that an element contains important or time-sensitive information.

2. ARIA Attributes

ARIA attributes provide additional information about elements with ARIA roles. They help in describing the state, properties, or other relevant information. Here are some common ARIA attributes:

- `aria-label`: Provides a concise label for an element when the visible label is insufficient or absent.

- `aria-labelledby`: References the ID of another element that serves as the label for the current element.

- `aria-describedby`: References the ID of another element that provides additional descriptive information about the current element.

- `aria-hidden`: Indicates whether an element is visible or hidden to assistive technologies. It can take values like "true" or "false."

- `aria-expanded`: Indicates whether an element that can be expanded or collapsed is currently expanded or not.

- `aria-selected`: Indicates whether an element in a group of elements is selected.

3. Examples of ARIA Usage

Let's look at some examples of how ARIA roles and attributes can be used in HTML:

Example 1: ARIA button
```
<button role="button" aria-label="Close" onclick="closeDialog()">X</button>
```

In this example, we use `role="button"` and `aria-label` to indicate that the `<button>` element functions as a close button.

Example 2: ARIA menu
```
<nav role="menu">
  <ul>
    <li role="menuitem"><a href="/">Home</a></li>
    <li role="menuitem"><a href="/about">About</a></li>
    <li role="menuitem"><a href="/contact">Contact</a></li>
  </ul>
</nav>
```

Here, we use `role="menu"` and `role="menuitem"` to define a navigation menu.

Example 3: ARIA checkbox group
```
<fieldset role="group" aria-label="Toppings">
  <legend>Select Toppings</legend>
  <input type="checkbox" id="topping1" aria-label="Pepperoni">
  <label for="topping1">Pepperoni</label>
  <input type="checkbox" id="topping2" aria-label="Mushrooms">
  <label for="topping2">Mushrooms</label>
</fieldset>
```

In this example, we use ARIA roles and labels to create an accessible group of checkboxes.

4. Testing and Validation

It's essential to test the accessibility of your web content when using ARIA roles and attributes. Various web accessibility testing tools and browser extensions can help you identify any issues or errors related to ARIA usage. Additionally, ensure that your ARIA implementations are consistent with the functionality and behavior of your web application.

Incorporating ARIA roles and attributes into your web development process can significantly improve the accessibility of your web applications, making them more usable for individuals with disabilities and enhancing their overall user experience.

Section 18.4: SEO Best Practices

Search Engine Optimization (SEO) is a crucial aspect of web development and content creation. It involves optimizing your website's content and structure to improve its visibility and ranking in search engine results pages (SERPs). Effective SEO practices help drive organic traffic to your site and ensure that your content reaches a broader audience. In this section, we'll explore some essential SEO best practices.

1. Keyword Research

Keyword research is the foundation of SEO. It involves identifying the keywords and phrases that users are likely to use when searching for content related to your website. Several keyword research tools are available, such as Google Keyword Planner and Ahrefs Keywords Explorer. By selecting relevant keywords and strategically incorporating them into your content, you can increase your chances of ranking higher in search results.

2. High-Quality Content

Creating high-quality, informative, and engaging content is essential for SEO success. Search engines prioritize content that provides value to users. Ensure that your content is well-written, free of spelling and grammar errors, and formatted for readability. Additionally, regularly updating your content with fresh information can improve its ranking over time.

3. Meta Tags

Meta tags are HTML elements that provide information about a web page to search engines. Two important meta tags for SEO are:

- **Title Tag**: This tag defines the title of a web page and appears as the clickable link in search results. It should contain relevant keywords and accurately describe the page's content.

- **Meta Description**: The meta description provides a brief summary of the page's content. It should be concise, engaging, and include relevant keywords to entice users to click on your link.

```
<head>
    <title>Best SEO Practices - Your Website</title>
    <meta name="description" content="Learn essential SEO best practices to imp
rove your website's visibility in search engine results.">
</head>
```

4. Optimize Images and Media

Images and media files can enhance your content, but they should be optimized for SEO. Use descriptive file names and include alt text for images to provide context to search engines and assistive technologies. Compress images to reduce load times, which can impact your site's SEO.

```
<img src="image.jpg" alt="SEO Best Practices" />
```

5. Internal and External Links

Include internal links within your content to guide users to related pages on your website. External links to reputable sources can also improve your content's credibility. Ensure that your links are relevant and add value to the user's experience.

6. Mobile-Friendly Design

With the increasing use of mobile devices for web browsing, having a mobile-friendly design is crucial for SEO. Search engines prioritize mobile-responsive websites in their rankings. Use responsive design techniques to ensure your site adapts to various screen sizes.

7. Site Speed and Performance

Website speed is a ranking factor in search algorithms. Users expect fast-loading pages, so optimize your site's performance by minimizing HTTP requests, enabling browser caching, and using content delivery networks (CDNs).

8. XML Sitemap and Robots.txt

Create an XML sitemap to help search engines index your site's pages effectively. Additionally, use a robots.txt file to specify which parts of your site should or should not be crawled by search engine bots.

9. Regular Monitoring and Analysis

SEO is an ongoing process. Regularly monitor your site's performance using tools like Google Analytics and Google Search Console. Analyze data on organic traffic, keywords, and user behavior to identify areas for improvement.

10. Stay Informed

The field of SEO is constantly evolving. Stay updated with the latest SEO trends, algorithm changes, and best practices by following reputable SEO blogs and resources.

By implementing these SEO best practices, you can enhance your website's visibility, reach a broader audience, and provide a better user experience, ultimately contributing to the success of your web project.

Section 18.5: Optimizing for Search Engines

Optimizing your website for search engines (SEO) is an ongoing process that requires careful attention to various factors. In this section, we will explore some advanced SEO techniques and strategies that can help you improve your website's search engine ranking and visibility.

1. Voice Search Optimization

With the increasing use of voice-activated devices and virtual assistants like Siri and Alexa, optimizing your content for voice search is becoming crucial. Voice searches are often conversational and long-tail in nature. To optimize for voice search, focus on providing concise answers to common questions and using natural language in your content.

2. Featured Snippets

Featured snippets are selected search results that appear at the top of Google's SERPs in a box. They provide a concise answer to a user's query. To increase the chances of your content being featured as a snippet, structure your content in a way that directly answers common questions or provides solutions to problems.

3. Schema Markup

Schema markup is a type of structured data that you can add to your HTML to provide search engines with additional information about your content. This can enhance the way your content is displayed in search results. Schema markup can be used for various types of content, including articles, reviews, events, and more.

```
<script type="application/ld+json">
{
  "@context": "http://schema.org",
  "@type": "Article",
  "headline": "Advanced SEO Techniques",
  "datePublished": "2023-10-01",
  "description": "Learn advanced SEO techniques to boost your website's searc
h engine ranking.",
  "author": {
    "@type": "Person",
    "name": "Your Name"
  },
  "publisher": {
    "@type": "Organization",
    "name": "Your Company",
    "logo": {
      "@type": "ImageObject",
      "url": "https://www.example.com/logo.jpg"
    }
  }
}
</script>
```

4. Video SEO

If your website includes video content, optimizing it for search engines is essential. Use descriptive video titles, descriptions, and tags. Also, consider creating video transcripts to make your content more accessible and searchable.

5. Mobile-First Indexing

Google has adopted a mobile-first indexing approach, meaning it primarily uses the mobile version of your site for ranking and indexing. Ensure that your website is responsive and offers an excellent user experience on mobile devices.

6. Page Speed Optimization

Page speed continues to be a critical factor for SEO. Minimize image sizes, leverage browser caching, and enable compression to improve load times. Use tools like Google's PageSpeed Insights to identify and fix performance issues.

7. Local SEO

For businesses with physical locations, optimizing for local search is essential. Create and optimize your Google My Business listing, encourage customer reviews, and ensure that your business information is consistent across online directories.

8. Backlink Building

Building high-quality backlinks from reputable websites can significantly impact your SEO efforts. Focus on creating valuable and shareable content that naturally attracts backlinks. Avoid spammy link-building practices.

9. User Experience (UX) Optimization

A positive user experience contributes to lower bounce rates and higher search rankings. Ensure that your site is easy to navigate, has a clear layout, and offers fast-loading pages. Improve UX by addressing mobile responsiveness, reducing intrusive pop-ups, and optimizing site structure.

10. Content Freshness

Updating and adding new content to your website demonstrates its relevance and can positively affect SEO. Regularly revisit and refresh older content, and create new, engaging pieces to keep your site current and appealing to both users and search engines.

Incorporating these advanced SEO techniques into your website optimization strategy can lead to improved search engine rankings, increased organic traffic, and a more significant online presence. Keep in mind that SEO is an ongoing effort that requires monitoring, analysis, and adaptation to stay competitive in the digital landscape.

Chapter 19: Web Hosting and Deployment

In this chapter, we'll delve into the essential aspects of web hosting and deployment. Once you've created your website or web application, the next step is to make it accessible to the world. This involves selecting a web hosting provider, configuring your hosting environment, and deploying your content. We'll cover various topics related to web hosting, including domain name setup, SSL certificates for security, and ongoing maintenance.

Section 19.1: Choosing a Web Hosting Provider

Choosing the right web hosting provider is a critical decision for your online presence. Your hosting provider will determine the performance, reliability, and security of your website or application. Here are some factors to consider when selecting a web hosting provider:

1. Types of Hosting

- Shared Hosting: Suitable for small websites with low traffic. Your site shares server resources with other websites.

- Virtual Private Server (VPS) Hosting: Provides dedicated resources on a virtual server, offering better performance and customization options.

- Dedicated Hosting: Offers an entire server exclusively for your website or application, providing maximum control and performance.

- Cloud Hosting: Utilizes multiple servers in a network, ensuring scalability and high availability.

2. Performance and Reliability

- Check the provider's uptime guarantee. You want your site to be accessible to users at all times.

- Consider the server location. Hosting servers closer to your target audience can lead to faster loading times.

- Evaluate the provider's hardware, including the type of drives used (SSD for faster performance).

3. Scalability

- Ensure that the hosting plan can accommodate your future growth. Scalability is crucial as your website or application expands.

4. Support and Customer Service

- Look for a hosting provider with excellent customer support. They should offer multiple support channels, including live chat, email, and phone support.

5. Security Features

- Assess the security measures in place, such as firewalls, DDoS protection, and regular backups.

6. Price and Billing

- Compare pricing plans and check for any hidden fees.

- Pay attention to the renewal costs, as they can differ from the initial signup prices.

7. Control Panel and Ease of Use

- Ensure that the hosting provider offers an easy-to-use control panel for managing your hosting environment.

- Features like one-click installations for popular applications can be beneficial.

8. Reviews and Recommendations
- Read reviews and seek recommendations from other website owners or developers who have experience with the hosting provider.

9. Domain Name Services
- Some hosting providers offer domain registration services. Consider whether you want to register your domain with the same provider for convenience.

10. Scalability and Resources
- Evaluate the hosting provider's ability to accommodate your resource needs, including CPU, RAM, and storage.

Once you've considered these factors, you can make an informed decision about which web hosting provider is the best fit for your website or web application. Keep in mind that your hosting choice can significantly impact your site's performance, security, and overall success, so take your time to research and choose wisely.

Section 19.2: Uploading Your Website

Once you've selected a web hosting provider and set up your hosting environment, the next step is to upload your website or web application to the hosting server. This process involves transferring your website files, databases, and other assets from your local development environment to the remote server. In this section, we'll explore the methods and tools you can use to upload your website effectively.

Uploading Methods

There are several methods you can use to upload your website to a web hosting server. The choice of method often depends on your hosting provider's offerings and your familiarity with different tools. Here are some common uploading methods:

1. FTP (File Transfer Protocol)
- FTP is one of the most traditional and widely used methods for uploading files to a web server. You'll need an FTP client (e.g., FileZilla, Cyberduck) to connect to your hosting server using your FTP credentials.

- Once connected, you can navigate the server's file structure and transfer files between your local machine and the server by dragging and dropping.

- FTP is suitable for small to medium-sized websites, but it may not be the most efficient method for large-scale applications.

Example FTP upload using FileZilla:

```
# Connect to the server
Host: your-hosting-provider.com
Username: your-ftp-username
Password: your-ftp-password

# Transfer files by dragging and dropping
```

2. SFTP (Secure File Transfer Protocol)

- SFTP is a secure version of FTP that encrypts data during transmission, providing an extra layer of security. It's a recommended choice for sensitive data.

- The process of using an SFTP client is similar to FTP, but you'll connect using the server's SSH credentials.

Example SFTP upload using WinSCP:

```
# Connect to the server
Host name: your-hosting-provider.com
Port number: 22
Username: your-ssh-username
Password: your-ssh-password

# Transfer files securely
```

3. Web-based File Managers

- Some hosting providers offer web-based file managers within their control panels. These managers allow you to upload, download, and manage files directly through your web browser.

- While convenient, web-based file managers may have limitations in terms of functionality and file size limits.

4. Git and Version Control

- If your website or application is version-controlled using Git, you can push your code to a remote repository hosted on the server. Then, pull the changes on the server to deploy your site.

- This method is particularly useful for web developers who follow a version control workflow.

Example Git deployment:

```
# Push changes to remote Git repository
git push origin main

# Pull changes on the server
git pull origin main
```

Considerations for Uploading

Before uploading your website, consider the following best practices:

- **Backup**: Always have a local backup of your website files and databases before making any changes or uploads to the live server. This ensures you can recover your site in case of any issues.

- **File Permissions**: Ensure that file and directory permissions are correctly set on the server to avoid security vulnerabilities.

- **Database Migration**: If your website relies on a database, make sure to export and import the database to the server. Update your database configuration settings to connect to the remote database.

- **Testing**: After uploading, thoroughly test your website on the live server to ensure everything works as expected. Check for broken links, missing files, and any issues that may arise from differences between your local development environment and the server.

- **Content Delivery**: Consider using a Content Delivery Network (CDN) to serve static assets like images, stylesheets, and scripts from a location closer to your users, improving loading times.

- **Monitoring**: Implement website monitoring and tracking tools to keep an eye on the performance and uptime of your site. This helps you quickly identify and address any issues that may arise.

By following these guidelines and selecting the appropriate upload method, you can successfully deploy your website to a web hosting server, making it accessible to users worldwide. Be sure to keep your website files and databases up to date with any changes or updates you make to your site in the future.

Section 19.3: Domain Name Setup

After uploading your website to a web hosting server, the next crucial step is setting up a custom domain name. A domain name is the web address that users will use to access your site (e.g., www.example.com). This section will guide you through the process of acquiring and configuring a domain name for your website.

Domain Name Registration

To get a custom domain name, you typically need to register it through a domain registrar. Here are the steps to follow:

1. **Choose a Domain Name**: Select a unique and relevant domain name for your website. Consider a name that reflects your brand, content, or purpose. Keep it concise and memorable.

2. **Check Domain Availability**: Use the domain registrar's search tool to check if your desired domain name is available. If it's already registered, you may need to choose an alternative or try different domain extensions (e.g., .com, .net, .org).

3. **Select a Domain Extension**: Decide on the domain extension that best suits your website. The most common ones are .com, .net, and .org, but there are many others available.

4. **Register the Domain**: Once you've found an available domain name, proceed to register it through the registrar's website. You'll need to provide your contact information and agree to the registrar's terms and conditions.

5. **Domain Ownership**: After successful registration, you own the domain name for a specified period (usually one year). You can renew it annually to maintain ownership.

Domain Name Configuration

Configuring your domain name to point to your web hosting server involves setting up DNS (Domain Name System) records. These records determine where requests for your domain should be directed. Here's how to do it:

1. **Access Domain Registrar Settings**: Log in to your domain registrar's website and navigate to the domain management or DNS settings.

2. **Name Servers**: Most domain registrars use default name servers. However, if your hosting provider has specific name servers (e.g., ns1.yourhostingprovider.com), you'll need to update your domain's name server records to point to your hosting provider's servers.

   Example of updating name servers:

   ```
   Name Server 1: ns1.yourhostingprovider.com
   Name Server 2: ns2.yourhostingprovider.com
   ```

3. **A Record**: Create an A (Address) record that associates your domain name with the IP address of your web hosting server. This tells the DNS where to find your website.

   Example of configuring an A record:

   ```
   Host: @
   Type: A
   Value: Your_server_IP_address
   TTL: Default (or specify a time in seconds)
   ```

4. **CNAME Record** (Optional): If you want to set up subdomains (e.g., blog.example.com), you can use CNAME (Canonical Name) records to alias subdomains to your domain.

    Example of configuring a CNAME record:

    ```
    Host: blog
    Type: CNAME
    Value: Your_server_domain.com
    TTL: Default (or specify a time in seconds)
    ```

5. **MX Record** (Optional): If you want to use custom email addresses associated with your domain (e.g., contact@example.com), you'll need to configure MX (Mail Exchange) records for email delivery.

    Example of configuring an MX record:

    ```
    Host: @
    Type: MX
    Value: Your_mail_server_domain.com
    Priority: 10 (or as specified by your email provider)
    TTL: Default (or specify a time in seconds)
    ```

6. **Save Changes**: Save your DNS record changes. Note that DNS changes may take some time (up to 48 hours) to propagate across the internet.

Once your DNS records are updated, your domain name will point to your web hosting server. You can then access your website using your custom domain name.

SSL Certificate (HTTPS)

To enhance security and user trust, consider installing an SSL (Secure Sockets Layer) certificate for your domain. Many hosting providers offer free SSL certificates that enable HTTPS encryption, ensuring that data transmitted between users and your website is secure.

The process of obtaining and configuring an SSL certificate varies depending on your hosting provider. It often involves a few simple steps, including certificate generation, domain validation, and installation.

By following these steps, you can successfully set up and configure a custom domain name for your website, making it accessible to users under a professional and branded web address. Additionally, securing your site with HTTPS enhances security and user confidence in your online presence.

Section 19.4: SSL Certificates and Security

Securing your website is of paramount importance, not only for the safety of your visitors but also for search engine rankings and trustworthiness. In this section, we will explore the significance of SSL certificates and how to implement them for your website's security.

What is an SSL Certificate?

SSL (Secure Sockets Layer) is a standard security protocol for establishing encrypted links between a web server and a browser. SSL certificates are data files that bind a cryptographic key to the details of your website. When installed on a web server, they enable secure connections and encrypt sensitive data, such as login credentials, payment information, and personal details.

Why SSL is Important

1. **Data Security**: SSL encryption ensures that data transmitted between a user's browser and your web server remains confidential and secure. This is particularly important for e-commerce websites and any site that handles user data.

2. **Trust and Credibility**: Websites with SSL certificates display a padlock icon in the browser's address bar and use "https://" in their URLs. This signals to visitors that your site is trustworthy and their data is protected.

3. **SEO Benefits**: Search engines like Google prioritize secure websites in their search rankings. Having an SSL certificate can improve your website's visibility and SEO performance.

4. **Browser Compatibility**: Many modern browsers flag websites without SSL certificates as "Not Secure." This warning can deter visitors from staying on your site.

Obtaining an SSL Certificate

You can obtain an SSL certificate through various means:

1. **Hosting Provider**: Many hosting providers offer free SSL certificates as part of their hosting packages. Check if your hosting provider provides this service, and if so, how to enable it.

2. **Certificate Authorities (CAs)**: There are several trusted CAs, such as Let's Encrypt, Comodo, and DigiCert, that issue SSL certificates. Some offer free certificates, while others charge a fee. You can purchase a certificate directly from a CA and then install it on your web server.

Types of SSL Certificates

There are different types of SSL certificates, including:

1. **Domain Validated (DV) Certificates**: These are basic certificates that verify the domain ownership. They are easy to obtain and suitable for most websites.

2. **Organization Validated (OV) Certificates**: These certificates require more extensive validation of the domain owner's identity. They are ideal for businesses and e-commerce sites.

3. **Extended Validated (EV) Certificates**: EV certificates provide the highest level of trust and security. They involve a rigorous validation process and display the organization's name in the browser's address bar.

Installing an SSL Certificate

The process of installing an SSL certificate varies depending on your hosting provider and server type (e.g., Apache, Nginx, cPanel). Generally, it involves the following steps:

1. **Generate a Certificate Signing Request (CSR)**: You'll need to create a CSR on your server. This is a cryptographic file containing your server's public key.

2. **Submit CSR to CA**: If you purchase a certificate from a CA, you'll need to submit your CSR for validation. The CA will issue the SSL certificate after confirming domain ownership.

3. **Install the SSL Certificate**: Once issued, you'll receive the SSL certificate files. Install them on your server by following your hosting provider's or server software's instructions.

4. **Configure Your Server**: Update your server configuration to use the SSL certificate. This includes specifying the certificate file and private key file.

5. **Test and Verify**: After installation, thoroughly test your website to ensure SSL is working correctly. You can use online tools to check your SSL configuration.

6. **Update Website Links**: Ensure that all internal links and resources on your website use "https://" instead of "http://." This includes updating image links, style sheets, and scripts.

Renewing SSL Certificates

SSL certificates have a validity period, typically ranging from one to two years. It's essential to keep track of your certificate's expiration date and renew it in a timely manner. Most CAs and hosting providers offer automatic renewal options to simplify this process.

Conclusion

Implementing an SSL certificate is a crucial step in ensuring your website's security, building trust with visitors, and improving search engine rankings. Whether you choose a free or paid certificate, the benefits of SSL far outweigh the effort required to set it up. Prioritize the security of your website to protect both your users and your online reputation.

Section 19.5: Monitoring and Maintenance

Maintaining a website is an ongoing process that ensures its continued functionality, security, and performance. In this section, we'll delve into the importance of monitoring and maintaining your website to keep it running smoothly.

The Need for Monitoring and Maintenance

Websites are dynamic entities that can be affected by various factors over time. These factors include software updates, security vulnerabilities, changes in user behavior, and server performance. Failing to monitor and maintain your website can lead to issues such as downtime, security breaches, and a decline in user experience.

Key Aspects of Website Monitoring and Maintenance

1. **Software Updates**: Regularly update your website's software components, including the content management system (CMS), plugins, themes, and server software. Outdated software can be vulnerable to security threats.

2. **Backup Systems**: Implement automated backup solutions to regularly back up your website's data and files. Backups are essential for recovering your site in case of data loss or a security incident.

3. **Security Checks**: Perform security scans and audits to identify and fix vulnerabilities. Implement security best practices, such as using strong passwords, restricting access, and monitoring for suspicious activity.

4. **Performance Optimization**: Regularly check your website's performance using tools like Google PageSpeed Insights. Optimize images, minimize code, and utilize content delivery networks (CDNs) to improve loading times.

5. **Content Updates**: Keep your website's content fresh and up-to-date. Regularly publish new content, update existing information, and remove outdated material. This not only benefits users but also improves SEO.

6. **Broken Links and Errors**: Use tools to identify broken links and errors on your website. Fixing these issues enhances user experience and SEO rankings.

7. **User Experience (UX) Testing**: Continuously test your website's UX by gathering user feedback, analyzing user behavior, and conducting usability tests. Make improvements based on these findings.

8. **Performance Monitoring**: Use monitoring tools to track website performance, uptime, and server resource usage. Set up alerts to be notified of any issues immediately.

9. **Mobile Responsiveness**: Ensure your website is responsive and functions well on various devices, including smartphones and tablets. Test and adjust the design as needed.

10. **Database Optimization**: If your website relies on a database, regularly optimize it to improve efficiency and reduce load times.

11. **Legal Compliance**: Ensure that your website complies with relevant laws and regulations, including data protection and accessibility standards.

Website Maintenance Schedule

Creating a maintenance schedule is crucial for keeping your website in top shape. Depending on your website's complexity and traffic, you may need to perform daily, weekly, monthly, or quarterly tasks. Here's a sample schedule:

- **Daily**: Check for security alerts, perform backups, and review website analytics.
- **Weekly**: Update software, scan for broken links, and check for 404 errors.
- **Monthly**: Optimize images, review content, and analyze SEO performance.
- **Quarterly**: Conduct security audits, test UX, and assess the need for server upgrades.

Documentation and Tracking

Maintain records of all maintenance activities, including the date, tasks performed, and outcomes. Documentation helps in troubleshooting and ensures that nothing is overlooked during future maintenance.

Conclusion

Website monitoring and maintenance are continuous processes that safeguard your website's functionality, security, and user experience. By implementing regular checks and staying proactive, you can ensure that your website remains a reliable and valuable resource for your audience. Prioritize maintenance to avoid potential issues and deliver an excellent online experience.

Chapter 20: Advanced HTML and Beyond

In this final chapter, we'll explore advanced concepts and technologies that go beyond the fundamentals of HTML. These topics represent the cutting edge of web development and open up exciting possibilities for creating dynamic, interactive, and feature-rich web applications.

Section 20.1: Custom HTML Data Attributes

HTML5 introduced the ability to add custom data attributes to HTML elements. These attributes allow developers to store extra information about an element without using non-standard attributes or polluting the class or ID names. Custom data attributes are prefixed with "data-" and can be accessed and manipulated via JavaScript. Here's how you can use them:

```
<div id="product" data-product-id="12345" data-price="49.99" data-in-stock="true"></div>
```

In this example, we've added custom data attributes to a `<div>` element to store information about a product. You can access these attributes using JavaScript:

```
const productElement = document.getElementById("product");

// Accessing custom data attributes
const productId = productElement.getAttribute("data-product-id");
const price = productElement.getAttribute("data-price");
const inStock = productElement.getAttribute("data-in-stock");

console.log(productId); // Outputs: "12345"
console.log(price); // Outputs: "49.99"
console.log(inStock); // Outputs: "true"
```

Custom data attributes are useful for passing data between HTML and JavaScript in a standardized way. They are commonly used in web applications to associate data with elements and make it easily retrievable for scripting purposes.

Leveraging Custom Data Attributes

Dynamic Content

Custom data attributes can be used to store dynamic content or configuration settings for elements on a page. For example, in a content management system, you could use data attributes to store metadata about articles or posts.

```
<article data-post-id="123" data-author="John Doe" data-published="2023-03-15">
  <!-- Article content goes here -->
</article>
```

Interactive Elements

Custom data attributes are valuable for creating interactive elements. You can use them to associate specific behaviors or data with elements like buttons, links, or interactive widgets.

```html
<button data-action="like" data-post-id="123">Like</button>
<button data-action="share" data-post-id="123">Share</button>
```

JavaScript Interaction

Custom data attributes simplify JavaScript interactions. You can use `dataset` to access these attributes directly.

```javascript
// Using dataset to access custom data attributes
const postId = buttonElement.dataset.postId;
const action = buttonElement.dataset.action;
```

Styling with CSS

Custom data attributes can also be leveraged in CSS for styling purposes. You can create CSS rules based on data attributes to apply specific styles to elements with certain data.

```css
/* Style buttons with data-action attribute */
button[data-action="like"] {
  color: #FF5733;
}

button[data-action="share"] {
  color: #007BFF;
}
```

Custom data attributes are a powerful tool in modern web development, enabling you to create more organized, interactive, and data-driven web applications. When used effectively, they enhance code readability, maintainability, and extensibility.

Section 20.2: Microdata and Schema.org

Microdata is a way to embed semantic markup in HTML content to provide additional context and meaning to web pages. This structured data format helps search engines and other web services understand the content and relationships between different pieces of information on a webpage. One of the most popular vocabularies used for microdata is Schema.org, which provides a wide range of schemas to describe various types of content.

Understanding Microdata

Microdata consists of key-value pairs that are added as attributes to HTML elements. These key-value pairs define properties and their values for specific items on a webpage. Items, in this context, can represent various entities such as products, events, people, organizations, and more.

Here's a basic example of microdata using Schema.org:

```
<div itemscope itemtype="http://schema.org/Person">
  <h1 itemprop="name">John Doe</h1>
  <p><span itemprop="jobTitle">Web Developer</span> at <span itemprop="affili
ation">ABC Inc.</span></p>
</div>
```

In this example, we've used the `itemscope` attribute to define a scope for the item (in this case, a person), and `itemtype` to specify the type of item, which is a person according to Schema.org. The `itemprop` attributes are used to define properties and their values within the item.

Benefits of Microdata

1. **Improved SEO**: Search engines can better understand the content of your web pages, leading to improved search engine rankings and more relevant search results.

2. **Rich Snippets**: Microdata can enable the display of rich snippets in search engine results, providing users with more information about your content.

3. **Structured Data**: It adds structure to your content, making it easier to parse and process by various applications.

4. **Accessibility**: Microdata can also benefit accessibility by providing additional context for screen readers and other assistive technologies.

Using Schema.org

Schema.org provides a comprehensive vocabulary for describing a wide range of entities. Here are some common types of content that can benefit from Schema.org microdata:

- **Product**: Describe details about products, including name, description, price, availability, and more.

- **Event**: Provide information about events, such as date, time, location, and performers.

- **Person**: Describe individuals, including their name, job title, affiliation, and contact information.

- **Organization**: Provide details about organizations, including name, logo, contact information, and social profiles.

- **Article**: Describe articles, blog posts, news, and other written content with properties like headline, date published, and author.

Integrating Microdata

To integrate microdata into your web pages, you'll need to follow the Schema.org vocabulary and include the appropriate attributes (`itemscope`, `itemtype`, `itemprop`) in your HTML elements. Various tools and online validators are available to help you check your microdata for correctness and compliance with Schema.org.

In conclusion, microdata and Schema.org offer a powerful way to enhance the semantics of your HTML content. By providing structured data, you can improve your website's visibility in search engines, enable rich snippets, and make your content more accessible and understandable to both machines and humans.

Section 20.3: Web Components

Web Components are a set of web platform APIs that allow you to create custom, reusable, and encapsulated HTML elements. They enable you to build your own HTML tags with their own behavior, encapsulated styling, and reusability. Web Components consist of three main technologies: Custom Elements, Shadow DOM, and HTML Templates.

Custom Elements

Custom Elements allow developers to define their own HTML elements with custom behavior. These elements can encapsulate functionality and provide a clean, declarative way to add functionality to a webpage. Custom Elements are defined using JavaScript and the `customElements` API.

Here's a simple example of defining a custom element:

```
class MyCustomElement extends HTMLElement {
  constructor() {
    super();
    // Define the element's behavior here
  }
}

customElements.define('my-custom-element', MyCustomElement);
```

In this example, we define a custom element named `<my-custom-element>`. You can then use this element in your HTML like any other HTML tag.

Shadow DOM

Shadow DOM is a technology that allows you to encapsulate the styling and behavior of a web component. It provides a scoped, isolated DOM tree for a custom element, which means that styles and scripts within a Shadow DOM are contained within that element and won't affect or be affected by the surrounding page.

Here's an example of using Shadow DOM within a custom element:

```
class MyCustomElement extends HTMLElement {
  constructor() {
    super();
    const shadow = this.attachShadow({ mode: 'open' });
    // Create a shadow DOM and add elements to it
    shadow.innerHTML = `
      <style>
        /* Encapsulated CSS styles */
        :host {
          display: block;
          border: 1px solid #ccc;
          padding: 16px;
        }
      </style>
      <p>This content is encapsulated in Shadow DOM.</p>
    `;
  }
}

customElements.define('my-custom-element', MyCustomElement);
```

In this example, the `<style>` tag contains styles that apply only to the custom element and won't leak out to the rest of the page.

HTML Templates

HTML Templates allow you to define reusable chunks of HTML that can be cloned and inserted into the DOM when needed. They are especially useful when building Web Components, as they provide a way to define the structure of your component's template.

Here's an example of using an HTML Template:

```
<template id="my-template">
  <style>
    /* Encapsulated CSS styles */
    :host {
      display: block;
      border: 1px solid #ccc;
      padding: 16px;
    }
  </style>
  <p>This content is encapsulated in an HTML Template.</p>
</template>
```

You can then use JavaScript to clone and insert this template into the DOM.

Web Components are a powerful way to create reusable and encapsulated components for web applications. They provide a standard way to build custom elements with encapsulated styles and behavior, making it easier to maintain and extend web applications. As browser support for Web Components grows, they are becoming an essential tool for web developers looking to build modular and maintainable web applications.

Section 20.4: WebAssembly and HTML Future

WebAssembly (often abbreviated as WASM) is a binary instruction format designed to run alongside JavaScript in web browsers. It is a low-level, assembly-like language that allows high-performance execution of code on web pages. WebAssembly is designed to be a portable target for the compilation of high-level programming languages like C, C++, and Rust, enabling web developers to build more complex and computationally intensive web applications.

How WebAssembly Works

WebAssembly is executed in a virtual machine (VM) within the browser, and it provides a secure and efficient way to run code on web pages. Here's a simplified overview of how WebAssembly works:

1. Compilation: Developers write code in a high-level language like C or Rust. This code is then compiled into WebAssembly bytecode using specialized compilers.

2. Loading: The compiled WebAssembly module is loaded into the browser alongside the JavaScript code.

3. Execution: The WebAssembly module runs within a secure and isolated execution environment called the WebAssembly VM. It has access to a subset of the browser's APIs and interacts with JavaScript through a defined interface.

4. Interoperability: WebAssembly can call JavaScript functions and vice versa, allowing seamless integration with existing web code.

WebAssembly provides several benefits:

- **Performance**: WebAssembly executes code faster than JavaScript, making it suitable for tasks requiring high computational power.

- **Portability**: Since WebAssembly is a binary format, it can be easily shared and executed across different platforms and browsers.

- **Security**: WebAssembly runs in a sandboxed environment, ensuring that it doesn't have direct access to the user's system.

- **Interoperability**: WebAssembly can interact with JavaScript code, enabling developers to gradually introduce it into existing web applications.

HTML continues to evolve, and the future of web development looks promising with various emerging technologies and standards. Some key trends and developments include:

1. **Web Components**: As discussed in the previous section, Web Components are becoming a fundamental part of web development, allowing developers to create reusable and encapsulated components.

2. **Progressive Web Apps (PWAs)**: PWAs are web applications that offer a native app-like experience, including offline capabilities and push notifications. They are expected to become more prevalent.

3. **WebAssembly**: WebAssembly is likely to play a more significant role in web development, enabling developers to build high-performance web applications.

4. **WebVR and WebXR**: Virtual reality (VR) and augmented reality (AR) are gaining traction on the web. WebVR and WebXR APIs allow developers to create immersive experiences for users.

5. **Accessibility**: Web accessibility standards and practices will continue to be a focus, ensuring that web content is usable by people with disabilities.

6. **Web Security**: With an increasing number of online threats, web security will remain a top priority. Technologies like Content Security Policy (CSP) will help mitigate risks.

7. **Web Standards**: HTML, CSS, and JavaScript will continue to evolve through the efforts of standards organizations like the World Wide Web Consortium (W3C).

In conclusion, the future of HTML and web development is exciting and filled with opportunities. As technology continues to advance, web developers must stay up to date with the latest trends and standards to create compelling and accessible web experiences for users worldwide.

Section 20.5: Staying Updated in the HTML World

In the ever-evolving world of web development, staying updated is crucial. HTML, along with CSS and JavaScript, is at the core of web development, and new features, standards, and best practices are continually emerging. Here's how you can keep yourself informed and up-to-date in the HTML world:

1. **Follow Official Documentation**: The World Wide Web Consortium (W3C) is responsible for HTML standards. Keep an eye on their official website for the latest HTML specifications and updates. This is where you'll find the most accurate and authoritative information.

2. **Web Development Blogs**: Numerous web development blogs and websites regularly publish articles about HTML and related technologies. Some popular ones include MDN Web Docs, Smashing Magazine, and CSS-Tricks. Subscribe to their newsletters or RSS feeds to receive updates.

3. **Social Media and Forums**: Follow web development experts, organizations, and communities on platforms like Twitter, Stack Overflow, and GitHub. Participate in discussions, ask questions, and share your knowledge.

4. **Online Courses and Tutorials**: Platforms like Coursera, edX, Udemy, and freeCodeCamp offer courses on web development topics, including HTML. Enroll in relevant courses to learn new skills and stay updated.

5. **Webinars and Conferences**: Attend webinars, conferences, and meetups related to web development. These events often feature talks by industry experts and provide opportunities to network with other developers.

6. **GitHub Repositories**: Many open-source projects related to web development are hosted on GitHub. Explore and contribute to projects that interest you. It's an excellent way to gain practical experience.

7. **Experiment and Build Projects**: The best way to learn is by doing. Experiment with HTML, try out new features, and build personal projects. This hands-on experience will deepen your understanding.

8. **Browser Developer Tools**: Modern web browsers come with robust developer tools that can help you understand and debug HTML, CSS, and JavaScript. Familiarize yourself with these tools to become a more effective developer.

9. **Online Communities**: Join web development forums, subreddits, and online communities like Dev.to and Hashnode. Engage in discussions, seek advice, and share your experiences.

10. **Version Control**: Learn to use version control systems like Git. It's an essential skill for collaborating with other developers and managing your codebase efficiently.

11. **Newsletters**: Subscribe to newsletters that curate web development news and resources. They can save you time by delivering relevant information directly to your inbox.

12. **Books**: Invest in web development books, especially those that focus on the latest HTML and web standards. Books provide in-depth knowledge and often serve as valuable references.

13. **Continuous Learning**: Web development is a continuous learning journey. Be open to learning new technologies and adapting to changes in the industry.

14. **Teach Others**: Teaching can be an effective way to solidify your understanding. Share your knowledge through blog posts, tutorials, or by mentoring others.

15. **Stay Inquisitive**: Keep a curious mindset. When you encounter a problem or a new technology, dive into it to understand how it works. Don't shy away from challenges.

Remember that the field of web development is dynamic, and what's popular today may change tomorrow. Being adaptable, curious, and proactive in your learning will help you thrive in the ever-evolving HTML world.

www.ingramcontent.com/pod-product-compliance
Lightning Source LLC
LaVergne TN
LVHW051326050326
832903LV00031B/3396